"Crouching Tiger"

"Crouching Tiger": Quality and its Implementation in the Indian and Irish Software Communities

By Brendan Keane

Edited by Ita Richardson and Mícheál ó hAodha

CAMBRIDGE SCHOLARS PUBLISHING

"Crouching Tiger:": Quality and its Implementation in the Indian and Irish Software Communities,
by Brendan Keane Edited by Ita Richardson and Mícheál ó hAodha

This book first published 2007 by

Cambridge Scholars Publishing

15 Angerton Gardens, Newcastle, NE5 2JA, UK

British Library Cataloguing in Publication Data
A catalogue record for this book is available from the British Library

ISBN 1-84718-326-3; ISBN 13: 9781847183262

TABLE OF CONTENTS

LIST OF TABLES

LIST OF FIGURES

APPENDICES

ACKNOWLEDGEMENTS

Thanks to the following websites for providing Free To Download Quality Pictures:

http://www.reflexstock.com/
Laptop image (Royalty Free)

https://www.cia.gov/library/publications/the-world-factbook/
National flag of Ireland, National Flag of India (Public Domain)

http://images.fws.gov/
Tiger image from U.S. Fish and Wildlife Services (Public Domain).

PREFACE

The Irish software industry has blossomed within the past decade making Ireland one of the leading software nations in the world. Once a country whose primary industries were agriculture and manufacturing, Ireland has become a focal point for many multinational corporations setting up major offshore software bases. India, which is another country experiencing economic growth, modernisation and transition, is also considered an attractive, viable and low-cost outsourcing alternative for new software development companies. India has now risen to become one of the largest business-process outsourcing destinations in the world. Both Ireland and India hold in common that their respective economies can boast English speaking, well-trained and well-educated workforces. More importantly still – in the case of India – is the fact that it is a country which offers low labour costs and an apparent high focus on quality. Quality has become a vital marketing necessity in the global market place. Never before has the consumer had such a wide range of choice regarding what and where to buy, and software organisations have, as consequence, to continually improve the quality of their product if they wish to stay in business.

This volume explores the attitudes and experiences of the members of the Indian and Irish software communities towards quality. Research was first conducted in India over a three-month period and this was followed by a period of research within the Irish software industry. The results of this research are presented here, as is a comparison between the software industries of both countries with a focus on their use of quality as reflected through their implementation and experience of software quality models, in particular.

CHAPTER ONE

INTRODUCTION

1.1 Introduction

Although the Irish software industry been a rising star in the global software marketplace during the past twenty years, it has, as yet, to become one of the brightest in the sky. A new challenge for the Irish software industry and other European-based software companies generally has been the ongoing development of low-cost outsourcing destinations such as India. Not only has low-cost been a selling point for such countries, they have also focused on producing quality product through implementing measurable quality software processes. The purpose of this volume is to examine the attitudes and experiences of the members of the software communities of both Ireland and India towards software quality, with a specific focus on software processes.

Both the Irish and Indian software industries can boast a highly-educated and English-speaking workforce. The quality of products and services being offered has also become paramount in recent times. Depending on the product or service being provided, customers need never actually meet the provider who can potentially be on the opposite side of the globe. It is vital therefore that the product or service provider can give some kind of guarantee as to the quality of their product.

An acceptable measure by many customer organisations is for providers to demonstrate that the processes used in the creation or maintenance of the product or service are mature and capable of meeting the requisite needs of the customer. This is done through the implementation of measurable and certifiable software quality models. Certification by an independent body using internationally-recognised criteria can give customers assurances as to the quality of their provider's product or service. Product or service providers can also use certification as a marketing tool to attract more customers.

By exploring the attitudes and experiences of software development companies in India and Ireland it is hoped to gain an insight into how seriously the Irish and Indian software industries are taking the matter of software process quality. From this research we developed recommendations for the Irish software community as to how they may compete with Indian and other low-cost software providers.

It is worth mentioning here that while outsourcing now plays a major role in the software sector, this research is not focused on the merits, drawbacks or significance of outsourcing. Outsourcing is merely another factor which challenges the Irish software industry.

Elements of this research should prove beneficial not only to members of the Irish software industry, but to software industries of other countries which are all seeking to improve the quality of their product. It is also hoped that this research will provide useful information to the small-to-medium (SME) software organisations, which may not have the necessary skills or resources available to investigate their progress in the software quality sphere - where they are at, or where they ought to be, in terms of their own attitudes towards software process quality.

1.2 Research Summary

This volume examines attitudes and experiences towards quality through research undertaken with members of the software industries of both India and the Republic of Ireland.

Quality Review

Different opinions and theories regarding the concept of quality and Quality Management Systems are presented. This leads to a discussion of a number of varying approaches to quality as applied in the traditional sense of the word. These latter approaches to quality are taken from the perspective of three world-renowned authorities in the subject. The concept of Software Process Improvement (SPI) is then introduced, and various approaches to SPI in the form of particular software quality models – (sometimes referred to as software process models) – are then discussed.

Research Process

Research was conducted within the software industries of India and the Republic of Ireland. The aim of this research was to explore the opinions and the experiences of a sample of the members of the respective software communities towards quality and quality processes. The questions that this research attempts to answer are: What are the attitudes and experiences of software professionals in India and Ireland towards quality, and how do these attitudes and experiences compare?

Attitudes and Experience of Quality

A case study approach was adopted for this research and a series of interviews in India in collaboration with a large process consulting organization yielded a variety of useful research data. The results of this phase of the research are discussed, preceded by a general introduction to the Indian software industry. In Ireland, interviews were carried out with members of the Irish software community and data from an on line questionnaire was made available to the author. The analysis of this information is presented along with an introduction to the Irish software industry. Specific comparative analysis that was conducted between the two research phases within the area of software quality models is also discussed.

Conclusion

The conclusion is divided into three separate subject areas. The first area is a summary of this volume itself. Secondly a conclusion to the research into the examination of attitudes and experiences towards quality is presented. Finally, various recommendations to the Irish software industry, as based on the research undertaken, are presented. These recommendations are aimed primarily towards the small-to-medium (SME) software organisations in Ireland but are applicable to all software organizations in Ireland, irrespective of size.

Table 1.1 below presents the structure of the volume in graphical form and as divided into chapters and subsequent sections.

Table 1.1 Structure of this Volume

Chapter 1	*Chapter 2*	*Chapter 3*	*Chapter 4*	*Chapter 5*	*Chapter 6*	*Chapter 7*
Introduction	**Literature Review**	**Research Methodology**	**Indian attitudes towards quality**	**Irish attitudes towards quality**	**Focus on Quality: India and Ireland**	**Conclusion**
Sections	*Sections*	*Sections*	*Sections*	*Sections*	*Sections*	*Sections*
Research Introduction	What is Quality?	Introduction	Indian Software Industry	Irish Software Industry	Introduction	Summary of Thesis
Structure of this Volume	Quality Management Systems	Research Methods	Research Findings	Research Findings	Software Quality Models	Attitudes towards Quality
	Approaches to Quality	Research in India			Focus on Quality	Advice to Small Firms in Ireland
	What is Software Quality?	Change in Focus				Conclusion
	Software Process Improvement	Research in Ireland				
	Software Quality Models					

CHAPTER TWO

LITERATURE REVIEW

2.1 What is Quality?

Before the concept of software quality can be addressed, it is necessary to examine its origins in the form of quality in the traditional sense. But what exactly is quality? In simple terms, quality is the "degree of excellence" that is attributed to a product or service (Webster, 2003). Although this definition appears to answer the question "what is quality", it also raises several issues that must be dealt with before moving on. Quality is not a physical entity that can be seen or touched; yet for the most part it is obvious when quality is present and when it is missing or absent. Kitchenham states that quality is "hard to define, impossible to measure, easy to recognize" (Kitchenham, 1996).

The perception of quality varies depending on the situation. Weinberg (1991) says that quality is 'that' which gives a product its value. He goes on to say that the value of a product or service is the price that a customer is willing to pay for that product or service. Some people may value the same product or service differently; therefore the quality of the product depends on the individual's perception of that product or service at the time of use.

Sanders and Curran (1994) agree with Weinberg's statement saying "quality means different things to different people", and they go on to say in simple terms: "quality means satisfying customers". Each customer may have different needs, different preferences and a different social background; therefore a quality product or service means something different to each of them.

For example, the views of a millionaire and the views of a homeless person would probably differ over what counts as a quality bed. Whereas the millionaire would view the four-poster bed in the presidential suite of a 5-Star hotel as a quality product, the homeless person might view the bunk in the nearest homeless shelter as quality. Both beds provide the same essential function i.e. a sheltered place to sleep; both individuals view their respective beds as quality products; yet there is an obvious gap in the comfort and surroundings between both individuals.

2.1.1 Definitions of Quality

Over the years, even the foremost authorities on quality have had slightly different views on what quality actually is. It is worth noting that these three authorities mentioned below all formed their theories with the manufacturing industry in mind.

- Dr. Joseph M. Juran - a man of his time – who has variously been called the "father" of quality, a quality "guru" and the man who "taught quality to the Japanese", defines quality as *fitness for use*. i.e. Is the product capable of carrying out those functions for which it was intended? (Juran, 1979)
- Dr. William Deming, author of the book "Out of the crisis" defines quality as *conformity and dependability*. i.e.: Does the product meet its requirements and is it reliable in its functions (Deming, 1986).
- Philip Crosby, author of the famous book "Quality is Free" and of "Reflections on Quality" defines quality as *conformance to requirements* – similar to Deming's definition, relating quality to the ability of the product (or service) to do that which it was designed to do (Crosby, 1979).

The International Organization for Standardization (ISO) define quality as "The totality of features and characteristics of a product or service that bare on its ability to meet stated or implied needs" (ISO, 1986). The ISO definition, as well as Juran, Deming and Crosby's definitions focus on the ability of the product or service to meet its requirements. This raises the question – is quality just about meeting the requirements defined by the users or designers or are there other types of quality that can be considered when determining the "degree of excellence" of a product or service? Also, who determines what is to be considered a quality product or service?

Some other common definitions of quality include:

- **Quality of Design**: The appropriateness of the products' design and the specifications for its intended use.
- **Quality of Conformance**: The degree to which goods and services are consistent with the intent of the design. Influenced

by the capability of equipment, the training and skills of employees, worker motivation, and management commitment.

- **Quality of Performance**: The reliability of the original product or service as well as the competence and promptness of staff and support services.

Garvin (1984) gave five diverse yet somewhat-similar definitions of quality, justifying each definition according to the various different approaches or views as to what quality really is or who determines it. These five definitions and a brief explanation are provided here:

1. Transcendent Definition
   The quality of something is viewed as its natural excellence. Quality is an unanalysable property. Quality is neither mind nor matter, but a third entity independent of the two… even though quality cannot be defined, you know what it is.

2. Product-Based Definition
   The quality of a product is determined by the presence or absence of certain attributes or characteristics. Differences in quality amount to differences in the quantity of some desired ingredient or attribute.

3. User-based Definition
   The quality of a product depends on the products fitness for use in a particular application. Quality consists of the capacity to satisfy wants. Quality is fitness for use.

4. Manufacturing-Based Definition
   Quality is judged by the ability of a system to meet the requirements set down for it. Quality means conformance to requirements. Quality is the degree to which a specified product conforms to a design or specification.

5. Value-Based Definition
   Quality is the degree of excellence at an acceptable price and the control of variability at an acceptable cost. Quality means what is best for certain customer conditions. These conditions are (a) the actual use and (b) the selling price of the product.

In his book *Software Quality: Theory and Management* (1992) Alan Gillies states that: "Quality is determined by people because:

- It is people and human organizations who have problems to be tackled by computer software
- It is people who define the problems and specify the solutions
- It is still (currently) people who implement these designs and produce code
- It is people who test code
- It is people who use the final systems and will make judgements about the overall quality of the solution." (Gillies, 1992)

The researcher concludes that the quality of a product or service is determined by an individual's perception of how valuable the product or service can be to them in a particular situation. Quality is driven by the customer; it is they who determine what exactly quality is – according to their particular needs – and it is they who demand the highest standards at the lowest price.

2.2 Quality Management Systems

A Quality Management System (QMS) can be described as the collection of the processes and resources available to those organizations, which work together to improve and manage the quality of a product/service. According to (Sanders and Curran, 1994), the term "Quality System", or "Quality Management System" is used internationally to describe a process which ensures and demonstrates the quality of the products and services it produces. One of the most famous and simplistic Quality Management Systems is Edward Deming's "Deming Cycle of continuous improvement" (Figure 2.1), which he developed by building upon the work of Walter Shewart.

Plan: Define objectives and determine how to achieve them.
Do: Create the necessary conditions to fulfil the objectives and execute the plan.
Study: Compare actual results with expectations.
Act: Determine any future action based on 'Study Phase'.
Figure 2.1. The Deming Cycle

Quality management is meant to ensure that as few as possible – (if any) - faults occur at any stage during or after the development process of a product/service. Quality management systems are meant to ensure that quality is built into the particular product/service rather than being tested into the product. Successful quality systems place great emphasis on early corrective action. It is much cheaper for the developer to correct errors early in the product life cycle (Sanders and Curran, 1994).

According to National Aeronautics and Space Administration (NASA), "an effective and efficient QMS is one that recognizes the need to continuously change and improve an organization's products and services as determined by system feedback, and corresponding management decisions". The purpose of a QMS is "to minimize the variability in the quality of an organization's products and services" (NASA, 2003).

ISO list eight quality management principles on which the quality management system standards of ISO 9000:2000 series are based. These principles are intended for use by senior management to guide their organizations towards improved performance. ISO's eight quality management principals are:

- *Customer focus:*
  Organizations depend on their customers and should therefore understand their current and future customer needs, meet their customer requirements and strive to exceed their customer expectations.
- *Leadership:*
  Leaders establish unity of purpose and the direction of the organization. They should create and maintain the internal environment in which people can become fully involved in achieving the organization's objectives
- *Involvement of people:*
  People at all levels are the essence of an organization and their full involvement enables their abilities to be used for the organization's benefit.
- *Process approach:*
  A desired result is achieved more effectively when activities and related resources are managed as a process.
- *System approach to management:*

Identifying, understanding and managing interrelated processes as a system contributes to the organization's effectiveness and efficiency in achieving its objectives.

- *Continual improvement:*
  Continual improvement of the organization's overall performance should be a permanent objective of the organization.
- *Factual approach to decision making:*
  Effective decisions are based on the analysis of data and information.
- *Mutually beneficial supplier relationships:*
  An organization and its suppliers are interdependent and a mutually beneficial relationship enhances the ability of both to create value (ISO, 2003c)

According to the ISO definition, a QMS must have the following five components:

- Organizational Structure
- Responsibilities
- Procedures
- Processes
- Resources

Table 2.1 gives a summary of the procedures required by a QMS. In order to improve quality you must first be able to measure and analyse the gap between the current performance and the desired performance.

Table 2.1. Procedures in a Quality Management System (Gillies, 1997)

Procedure	**Purpose**
Contract review	To ensure requirements are clearly established and met
Design control	To control and verify design of products or services
Document control	To control production of all documentation, to ensure document consistency
Purchasing	To ensure that all products and services purchased meet the organization's requirements
Customer supplies	To ensure that all products and services supplied by the customer meet the organization's requirements
Traceability	To identify and trace materials from raw materials to finished product
Process control	To ensure sufficient instructions for any process required

Checking, inspecting, measuring and testing	To verify incoming products, 'in process' products, the finished product and test equipment
Nonconforming product or services	To document and segregate any nonconforming product or service
Corrective action	To provide corrective action to prevent nonconformity
Protection of quality	To prevent quality being eroded by incorrect handling, labelling or packing
Training	To identify, carry out and document necessary training
Statistical process control	To use SPC techniques to gather and analyse information on the state of control and capability
Quality system audit	To ensure the QMS is being carried out according to documented procedures

It is clear that the general consensus is the following: - To have an effective QMS an organization one must have the right people and the right attitude. Employees should be highly-trained and well-educated and senior management must be fully committed to the improvement of quality within the organization and not compromise quality against quantity when under pressure from demanding customers.

2.3 Approaches to Quality

In a previous section we came across three of the foremost authorities on quality - Deming, Juran and Crosby - and their definitions of quality. These three played an important role in the development of quality management as a means to improve product quality. Each of these authorities on the subject had their own particular approach. This section reviews their approaches to the issue of quality.

The idea of quality and of improving the quality of a product has been around for quite some time. Buzzwords such as "Quality Management" and "Quality Management Systems" encapsulate the idea of an 'approach' to quality. "Quality management" is essentially what an organization does to ensure that its products and/or services meet the expected requirements, as laid out by the customer. The subject area that is quality management can be traced back to the 1920s and 1930s and to the work of Shewart. He originated the idea of the plan-do-check/study-act with his 'Learning and Improvement Cycle' This was later built upon by Deming when it became known as the Deming Cycle.

2.3.1 Edward Deming's approach to quality

Deming is credited with extending and developing Shewart's initial research and ideas into the concept that is currently termed Total Quality Management (Casey, 2000). His approach necessitated that quality improvement lay in the ability to control and manage systems and processes properly and he firmly believed that quality should be orientated around the customer. He was also noted as a strong believer in employee participation in the decision-making process. He placed a strong emphasis on the necessity for senior management to take responsibility in ensuring the success of any quality improvement process and he continues to be an advocate of Statistical Process Control (SPC) as a means of improvement and the removal of variation within particular processes (Gillies, 1992).

Deming proposed 14 points for the management of quality as listed in the table below (See table 2.1). He believed that these points should be adhered to internally as well as externally by the suppliers of products and services to the organization in question. He believed in having a narrow field of suppliers, the idea being that a good relationship with a few select suppliers is far more beneficial than having a poor relationship with a larger number of suppliers. He also advocated the sharing of knowledge and various techniques especially especially as relating to SPC and suppliers - in the hope of ensuring the quality of the incoming supplies (Deming, 1986).

Table 2.2 Edward Deming's 14 points for quality management

1. Constancy of purpose
2. A new philosophy
3. Cease dependence on inspection
4. End lowest tender contracts
5. Improve every process
6. Improve training on the job
7. Institute leadership
8. Drive out fear
9. Break down barriers
10. Eliminate exhortations
11. Eliminate targets
12. Permit pride of workmanship
13. Encourage education
14. Create top management structures

2.3.2 Joseph M. Juran's approach to quality

Juran's approach to quality and his view of quality are similar to those of Deming. Juran believes that "quality does not happen by accident; it must be planned" (Bendell, 1998) in order for it to be a success and supporting this idea, he developed a quality 'structure' called Company Wide Quality Management (CWQM), where everyone from the top down must be fully committed to improving quality within the organization. Without this commitment from the very top, quality improvement methods are doomed to, at best, half hearted success and, at worst, complete failure (Juran, 1979).

Juran places quality planning in a quality trilogy which includes:

- Quality planning
- Quality control
- Quality improvement

His 'Quality Planning Road Map' consists of the following steps:

1. Identify who are the customers
2. Determine the needs of those customers
3. Translate those needs into our language
4. Develop a product that can respond to those needs
5. Optimise the product features so as to meet our needs as well as customer needs
6. Develop a process which is able to produce the product
7. Optimise the process
8. Prove that the process can produce the product under operating conditions
9. Transfer the process to Operation (Juran, 1988).

Again, similar to Deming, Juran's approach to quality management and improvement advocates the use of SPC. His approach is very people-oriented. He advocates teamwork, not only for low-level employees but also for senior management. He believes strongly in appropriate training and his methods are goal-oriented. His work focuses on people and processes and he realises the need for external customers and suppliers to place a high importance on quality (Gillies, 1997). Listed in table 2.3 are Juran's 10 points for quality management (Juran, 1979).

Table 2.3 Juran's 10 points for quality management

1. Build awareness of need and opportunity
2. Set goals for improvement
3. Organise to reach goals
4. Provide training
5. Carry out projects to solve problems
6. Report progress
7. Give recognition
8. Communicate results
9. Keep score
10. Maintain momentum by making annual improvement part of the regular process of the company

2.3.3 Philip Crosby's approach to quality

Crosby's approach to quality focuses on prevention as a means of achieving quality. He is best known for his book *Quality is Free* (1979) and is associated with the terms "Zero Defects", "Conformance to Requirements", "Four Absolutes of Quality" and "Quality Vaccine". By "Zero Defects" he does not mean that people never make mistakes, but that a company should not begin by expecting mistakes to be made and schedule additional 'just-in-case' products (Bendell, 1998). Crosby stressed that for any quality process to succeed, senior management must be fully committed to it. He also believed that a good understanding of quality, right across the board, was necessary to implement a successful quality improvement process. To achieve this, he believed in educating not only the workers but also the management as to the importance of quality and of the 'doing it right the first time' approach.

Crosby suggests a three-point 'quality vaccine' intended to prevent non-conformance:

1. Determination,
2. Education,
3. Implementation

Crosby also proposes the following four 'absolutes' of quality:

1. Definition: Conformance to requirements – Once requirements have been specified, quality is judged on whether they have been met or not.

2. System: Prevention, not test and fix – Prevention is better and cheaper than the cure.
3. Performance: Zero defects – The goal should be nothing less than perfect quality.
4. Measurement: The price of non-conformance – The cost spent on preventative measures should far outweigh that which is spent on fixing failures (Crosby, 1979).

Crosby also proposed 14 steps to quality improvement as show in table 2.4 below.

Table 2.4. - Crosby's 14 steps to quality improvement (Gillies, 1997)

1. Make it clear that management is committed to quality
2. Form quality improvement teams with each department represented
3. Determine where current and potential problems lie
4. Evaluate the cost of quality and explain its use as a tool
5. Raise the quality awareness and concern of all employees
6. Take action to correct identified problem
7. Establish a committee for the 'zero defects' programme
8. Train supervisors to actively carry out their role in quality improvement
9. Hold a 'zero defects day' for all employees to highlight the changes
10. Encourage individuals to establish improvement goals.
11. Encourage communication with management about obstacles to improvement
12. Recognize and appreciate participants
13. Establish quality councils to aid communication.
14. Do it all over again to show it never ends

Crosby stresses the need for continuous improvement. Crosby identifies 'quality building' tools including the Quality Management Maturity Grid (QMMG) (Crosby, 1979). The QMMG specifies five stages of maturity and their measurement categories (Casey, 2000) which enables a company to measure its current quality position. The QMMG formed the basis for the CMM Maturity Framework, which is described later in this section. An example of a Quality Management Maturity grid can be found in Appendix A.

From examining the approaches of Deming, Juran and Crosby to quality, it is clear that while they may have some differing ideas on how to approach quality management, they all point in the same direction, in the final analysis. Their differences lie in the approaches they each take. Deming's perspective is strongly user-based, believing that the only definition of quality that really matters is that of the customers. Juran's perspective is driven from the manufacturing/engineering point of view and is based strongly on planning for quality. Crosby's perspective is more management-focused – i.e. are the goals of quality being met and at what price?

2.4 What is Software Quality?

If the quality of a product or service can be defined as the "degree of excellence" of that product or service, then what is software quality? Could it simply be the "degree of excellence" of a software product or service? Yes it can, but how can this "degree of excellence" of a software product or service be measured? If software quality can be described as conformance to requirements, then can it be measured by the ability of the software product or service to meet the requirements of the customer? Yes it can. If software quality is measured through its dependability, does it mean that if the software product or service does not crash – (or is not temporarily unavailable) - it is then considered to be of high quality? Yes it does.

Conformance to requirements, dependability, fitness for use, maintainability and defects per thousand lines of code, are all among the factors that are considered when ascribing a quality status to a particular software product or service. It is safe to say that all of these factors contribute to the overall quality of a software product or service. It then stands to reason that the quality of a software product or service is dependent on the quality of each and every step involved in providing this product or service to a customer.

The ISO definition for quality mentioned earlier focused on the totality of features and characteristics of a product and their ability to meet stated needs. However, the quality of a software product or service is determined not only by the ability of individual features or characteristics to meet requirements, but by the quality of the processes used to develop these features and characteristics.

It may be possible to look at each individual product feature or characteristic and tweak each one so as to seek an improvement, but this approach would be neither efficient nor the best method of improving the overall product. A more efficient way of improving the quality of a software product or service is to improve the processes used to develop that particular product or service. Software Process Improvement (SPI) techniques and models are a tested and proven method for improving the quality of a process used to develop a software product or service.

2.5 Software Process Improvement

A process can be defined as:

- A sequence of activities that lead to some conclusion.

OR

- A logical organization of people, technology, and practices into work activities designed to transform information, materials, and energy into a specified end result (Pall, 1987).

The definition of a software process does not differ greatly from this. In fact (Humphrey, 1989) defines the software process as "the set of tools, methods and practices we use to produce a software product". Curtis et al (1993) expanded this further and defines a software process as "a set of activities, methods, practices and transformations that people use to develop and maintain software and the associated products".

SPI is essentially about improving the process of an evolving software product. This means that it tries to find ways of improving the existing practices and techniques in organizations that produce a software product, with a view to improving the overall quality of the software product, thereby increasing customer satisfaction. The needs and business goals of an organization are often centred on achieving enhanced customer satisfaction and greater competitiveness. It is these needs and requirements that determine the software process improvement goals that help to identify improvement actions and their priorities (SPICE, 1998c).

Richardson (1999) says that there is an emphasis placed on the software processes because companies expect that an improved software process will result in the improved quality of the software product. Paulk (1995a) states - "The quality of a software product is largely determined by the quality of the software development and maintenance processes used to build it". Zahran (1998) concurs with this belief and states "it is a widely accepted fact that the quality of a software product is largely determined by the quality of the process used to develop and maintain it".

SPI is best considered as a continuous improvement process, where an organization moves continually around an improvement cycle (SPICE, 1998c). Paulk, (1997) describes the Software Process Improvement Principle as: "The process to develop and maintain software that can be defined, managed, measured, and continuously improved". (Casey and Richardson, 2002) warn prospective dabblers in SPI saying that "SPI is a complex and expensive exercise, which should not be entered into lightly and without due preparation". The software process can be changed in "a series of steps or specific actions such by introducing new or changed practices into software processes or removing old ones" (SPICE, 1998c).

There are numerous methods and models used to implement software process improvement techniques. Models are used to help set process improvement objectives and priorities, improve processes, and provide guidance for ensuring stable, capable, mature processes. They provide an organization with:

- A place to start
- The benefit of a community's prior experiences
- A common language and a shared vision
- A framework for prioritising actions

(Phillips, 2002b)

Examples of such models are: the SEI's Capability Maturity Model (CMM), and Capability Maturity Model for Integration (CMMI), ISO's Software Process Improvement Capability determination (SPICE) initiative, in addition to quality standards such as the ISO 9000 series.

2.6 Capability Maturity Model

2.6.1 Background

In 1987, the Software Engineering Institute (SEI) from Carnegie Mellon University (CMU) released its description of a maturity framework. The intention of the CMM maturity framework was to provide the United States Department of Defence (US DoD) with an effective criteria to evaluate the maturity and capability of their software contractors (Paulk, Weber et al., 1995a). After four years of experience with the maturity framework, the SEI evolved the maturity framework into the Capability Maturity Model for Software (SW-CMM) (Paulk, Curtis et al., 1993). The SW-CMM defines a five-level framework for how an organisation matures its software process (Paulk, 1996). The model evaluates the software process within an organisation by measuring the level of process maturity and indicating its key weaknesses (Richardson, 1999).

The SW-CMM for software, provides software organisations with guidance on how to gain control of their processes for developing and maintaining software and how to evolve toward a culture of software engineering and management excellence (Paulk, Curtis et al., 1993). According to Casey (2000), CMM allows organisations to determine their current maturity level with reference to the model and provides a structured incremental path for the organisation to follow to improve their processes and reach higher maturity levels (Casey, 2000).

In 2000, the SEI began to upgrade to the Capability Maturity Model Integration and plans were underway to gradually phase out its support for the CMM. The CMM was due to be phased out by 2005. More information on the CMM, its structure, perceived strengths and weaknesses can be found in Appendix B.

2.7 Capability Maturity Model Integration (CMMI)

2.7.1 Introduction

Following the success of the CMM V1.1, it became clear that the generic nature of the CMM was applicable to other disciplines. The original CMM V1.1 became the CMM for software (SW-CMM), and four additional CMM-based models were developed:

- Software Acquisition CMM (SA-CMM)
- Systems Engineering CMM (SE-CMM)
- Integrated Systems Product & Process Development CMM (IPPD-CMM
- People CMM (P-CMM)

(Casey, 2000)

One of the problems associated with the previous CMM models was that there were so many of them as developed for a variety of disciplines. Mike Phillips, director of Special Projects at the Software Engineering Institute (SEI), says that "the use of multiple models has been expensive and complicated" (Phillips, 2002a). Each model had different structures, terms and ways of measuring maturity and it was therefore difficult to integrate them in a combined improvement program (Phillips, 2002b).

The Capability Maturity Model Integration research builds on and extends the principles initially embodied in the SW-CMM (SEI, 2002b). The CMMI is based on the SW-CMM Version 2.0 Draft, the SE-CMM, and the IPPD-CMM, and it addresses the problems mentioned above (Casey, 2000). The CMMI project integrates the systems and software disciplines into one process improvement framework, one which will allow for the introduction of new disciplines as needs arise (Phillips, 2002b).

2.7.1.1 Product Suite

The CMMI project has been developing a product suite including CMMI models, appraisal methods, and training materials since 1998. In January 2002 V1.1 was released which included CMMI models, training, and the Standard CMMI Appraisal Method for Process Improvement (SCAMPI^{SM}) (SEI, 2002c), see Table 2.5. In August, the SEI released the CMMI for Software (CMMI-SW) model and announced plans to develop CMMI interpretive guidance for software-only organizations (SEI, 2002c).

Table 2.5. The CMMI Product Suite

Models	Training	Appraisal Methods
Disciplines: • Systems Engineering • Software Engineering • Integrated Product and Process Development • Supplier Sourcing	Model: • Introduction to CMMI • Intermediate concepts	• Appraisal requirements for CMMI (ARC) • SCAMPI Method Description Document (MDD)
Representations: • Staged • Continuous	Instructor training Lead Appraiser	

The purpose of the CMMI Product Suite is to provide guidance for improving an organization's processes and its ability to manage the development, acquisition, and maintenance of products and services. The CMMI Product Suite places proven practices into a structure that helps an organization appraise its organizational maturity and process capability, establish priorities for improvement, and guide the implementation of these improvements (Heinz, 2002).

2.7.2 Structure of the CMMI

One of the criticisms levelled at the SW-CMM was its 'staged' nature. What this meant was that companies had to fulfil all KPA's from each level before being rated on the next level. For example, if a company had fulfilled all of the KPA's from levels 3 – 5, but was missing one KPA from level 2, the company could only be rated CMM level 2 compliant. One of the improvements that the CMMI framework offers is that it is capable of generating both staged and continuous representations of the capability models (Casey, 2000) .

The staged representation focuses on the organization as a whole and provides a road map of successive stages aimed at improving the organization's ability to understand and control its processes. The continuous representation focuses on individual processes, allowing the organization to choose which process or set of processes require more capability (Menezes, 2002). There are advantages to each model, but the decision to implement a particular model is dependent on the business needs of each individual organisation.

2.7.2.1 Continuous Model

Similar to the SW-CMM, the continuous model's summary components are process areas. Process areas are clusters of related practices, and are the building blocks in establishing process capability (Phillips, 2002b). Within each process area there are specific goals that are implemented by specific practices; there are also generic goals that are implemented according to more generic practices. Specific goals and practices are unique to individual process areas, whereas generic goals and practices apply to multiple process areas. Each practice belongs to only one capability level (Shrum, 2000). This is all similar to the SW-CMM. However, the major difference is that the levels of the continuous version of the model are cumulative, which means that higher capability levels include attributes of the lower levels (Phillips, 2002b). There are six levels:

5 – Optimising
4 – Quantitatively Managed
3 – Defined
2 – Managed
1 – Performed
0 – Incomplete

Figure 2.2 below shows the organization of Process areas as seen by the continuous representation of the model.

Category	Process Area
Project Management	Project Planning Project Monitoring and Control Supplier Agreement Management Integrated Project Management(IPPD) Integrated Supplier Management (SS) Integrated Teaming (IPPD) Risk Management Quantitative Project Management
Support	Configuration Management Process and Product Quality Assurance Measurement and Analysis Causal Analysis and Resolution Decision Analysis and Resolution Organizational Environment for Integration (IPPD)
Engineering	Requirements Management Requirements Development Technical Solution Product Integration Verification Validation
Process Management	Organizational Process Focus Organizational Process Definition Organizational Training Organizational Process Performance Organizational Innovation and Deployment

Figure 2.2. Continuous Organization of Process Areas (Phillips, 2002b)

Advantages of the continuous representation are:

- Provision of maximum flexibility for focusing on specific process areas according to business goals and objectives
- Familiar structure for those transitioning from the systems engineering community (Phillips, 2002b)
- High visibility of improvement within process areas
- Easy upgrade from EIA 731 (the systems engineering capability model)
- Easy comparison to ISO 15504 (SPICE – see section 2.9)
- Improvement of process areas can occur at different rates (Phillips, 2004)

2.7.2.2 Staged Model

In the staged representation, the summary components are maturity levels, where a maturity level is a well-defined evolutionary plateau on the path to becoming a mature organization. There are five maturity levels and each level is a layer in the foundation for continuous process improvement (Phillips, 2002b). Similar to the continuous representation the staged model has levels "1 – Performed" through to level "5 – Optimising". Figure 2.3 below shows the Process Areas in the staged representation model divided into their respective maturity levels.

Level	Focus	Process Areas
5 Optimizing	*Continuous process improvement*	Organizational Innovation and Deployment Causal Analysis and Resolution
4 Quantitatively Managed	*Quantitative management*	Organizational Process Performance Quantitative Project Management
3 Defined	*Process standardization* **(SS)** *(IPPD)* *(IPPD)*	Requirements Development Technical Solution Product Integration Verification Validation Organizational Process Focus Organizational Process Definition Organizational Training Integrated Project Management Integrated Supplier Management Risk Management Decision Analysis and Resolution Organizational Environment for Integration Integrated Teaming
2 Managed	*Basic project management*	Requirements Management Project Planning Project Monitoring and Control Supplier Agreement Management Measurement and Analysis Process and Product Quality Assurance Configuration Management
1 Performed		

Figure 2.3. Process Areas by Maturity Level (Phillips, 2002b)

Advantages of the staged representation include:

- Provides a roadmap for implementing:
    - Groups of process areas
    - Sequencing of implementation
- Familiar structure for those transitioning from the SW-CMM (Phillips, 2002b)
- Predefined and proven path with case study and ROI data
- Focuses on organizational improvement
- Easy upgrade from the SW-CMM
- Provides familiar benchmarking capability
- Overall results summarised in a maturity level (Phillips, 2004)

2.7.2.3 How to select a model?

When deciding which representation model to implement an organization should look at the comparative advantages and disadvantages of each, and decide which model is best suited for their organization. They then tailor the selected model to fit the organization and implement it. Roger Bate, principal architect of the CMMI Product Suite recommends three ways that an organization can reduce a model's size and complexity:

1. Select the right model. Once you select a model, tailor it to fit your organization's needs.
2. Don't try to implement the whole model at once. Select those parts that are most applicable and will have the biggest payoff at the first stage of process improvement - develop a base from which you can move forward.
3. Follow the practices that make the most sense for your organization. It is possible to pick and choose or substitute processes as long as they meet the overall goals (Heinz, 2002).

2.7.3 Benefits of the CMMI

In a special report focusing on the impact and benefits of CMMI, Goldenson and Gibson (2003) presented compelling evidence on the noted benefits that quality models such as CMMI can bring to organisations. The report focused on five separate areas of impact the CMMI has: Cost, schedule, quality, customer satisfaction and return on investment.

Cost benefits reported from CMMI include:

- 33% decrease in average cost to fix a defect (Boeing, Australia)
- 20% reduction in unit software costs (Lockheed Martin M&DS)
- Improved and stabilized Cost Performance Index (Northrop Grumman IT1)

Schedule benefits reported from CMMI include:

- Reduced by half the amount of time required to turn around releases (Boeing, Australia)
- Increased the percentage of milestones met from approximately 50% to approximately 95% (General Motors)
- 30% increase in software productivity (Lockheed Martin M&DS)

Quality benefits reported from CMMI include:

- Met goal of 20 +/- 5 defects per KLOC (Northrop Grumman IT1)

- Only 2% of all defects found in the fielded systems (Northrop Grumman IT1)
- Increased focus on quality by developers (Northrop Grumman IT1)

Customer satisfaction benefits reported from CMMI include:

- Increased award fees by 55% compared to an earlier SW-CMM baseline at maturity level 2 (Lockheed Martin M&DS)
- Received more than 98% of possible customer award fees (Northrop Grumman IT1)
- Earned a rating of "Exceptional" in every applicable category on their Contractor Performance Evaluation Survey (Northrop Grumman IT2)

Return on Investment (ROI) benefits reported from CMMI include:

- ROI for quality activities (Accenture)
- ROI calculated as defects avoided per hour spent in training and defect prevention (Northrop Grumman IT2)
- Process for earlier defect prevention, improved risk management, and better project control implemented after showing positive return on investment during pilot (Thales TT&S)

2.7.4 Concerns about CMMI

Four of the major concerns surrounding CMMI are:

- Perhaps it is just too big and too complex to be implemented
- It does not cater for small organizations
- It is relatively new
- Insufficient failure data

Regarding the size and complexity of the model, Roger Bate says: "the models are so lengthy because they provide comprehensive guidance and details". "It's similar to a dictionary," he says. "There are a lot of words in there that you'll never need to look up, but they're there so they can be available to everyone when and if they need them" (Bate cited in Heinz, 2002).

As for small organizations, Bate says that even though "the CMM models were developed in part to help larger organizations tackle complex issues across multiple disciplines, they can be tailored to meet the needs of smaller companies". He goes on to say that small organizations "don't need to commit to all the process areas and practices. CMMI is designed so they can pick and choose among the process areas that have the most immediate applicability to them" (Bate cited in Heinz, 2002).

Though CMMI is relatively new, it is built on the foundation of ideas dating back to 1979 and Crosby's Quality Management Maturity Grid, which matured into the Capability Maturity Model and eventually the Capability Maturity Model for Software, both software process models which were successfully tried and tested in organizations all over the world.

Reports on the benefits attributed to CMMI such as Goldenson and Gibson (2003) do much to assure potential users as to the positive impact CMMI can have. However what is missing from this report and others like it are examples and statistics regarding failures from implementing CMMI. Until such a time as credible data is available to document the reasons for these failures, reports concerning the benefits and the ROI of implementing process improvement initiatives may be passed over by sceptics – who may consider it as choosing it only because they consider it "the best of a bad bunch" (Keane and Richardson, 2004).

2.8 ISO 9000

2.8.1 Introduction

In 1987 the International Organization for Standardization (ISO) published its first set of standards known as the ISO 9000 series. The ISO 9000 family of standards represents an international consensus on good management practices with the aim of ensuring that the organization can, time and time again, deliver the product or services that meet the client's quality requirements (ISO/TC176, 2003b).

2.8.2 Structure of ISO 9000

When first published the ISO 9000 series consisted of five different, yet related standards that make ISO 9000 a quality system:

- ISO 9000: Quality management and quality assurance standards – guidelines for selection and use.
- ISO 9001: Quality systems – model for quality assurance in design/development, production, installation and servicing. This is a more detailed standard, which covers design, development,

production, installation, and servicing, this applies to the software industry.

- ISO 9002: Quality systems – Model for quality assurance in production and installation, which assesses the production and installation processes
- ISO 9003: Quality systems – Model for quality assurance in final inspection and test.
- ISO 9004: Quality management and quality systems elements – guidelines. (Dawood, 1994):

In December 2000, the ISO 9000 series was revised and several changes were made. An ISO publication at the time remarked that "The 2000 revisions of the ISO 9000 series represent the most thorough overhaul of these standards since they were first published in 1987" (ISO, 2000). The revisions were carried out by ISO Technical Committee 176 (ISO/TC 176), whose chairman, Dr. Pierre Caillibot, commented: "The new versions of the standards will provide organizations with an opportunity to improve their existing quality management systems with a view to adding value both for the organization and its customers" (ISO, 2000).

The changes include a reduction in the number of standards, more explicit requirements for achieving customer satisfaction and continual improvement (Kanholm, 1999). As can be seen from the table 2.7 below, the ISO 9000 series now consists of three core standards. The ISO 9000, ISO 9002 and ISO 9003 standards have been integrated into the new ISO 9001:2000 standard (ISO, 2002). Together these standards form the set of ISO's Quality Management System standards.

Table 2.6. ISO 9000:2000 standards, guidelines and purpose (ISO, 2003b)

Standards and Guidelines	**Purpose**
ISO 9000:2000, Quality management systems – Fundamentals and vocabulary	Establishes a starting point for understanding the standards and defines the fundamental terms and definitions used in the ISO 9000 family which you need to avoid misunderstandings in their use.
ISO 9000:2001, Quality management systems – Requirements	This is the requirement standard you use to assess your ability to meet customer and applicable regulatory requirements and thereby address the issue of customer satisfaction. It is now the only standard in the ISO 9000 family against which third-party certification can be carried.
ISO 9004:2000, Quality management systems – Guidelines for performance improvement	This guideline standard provides guidance for continual improvement of your quality management system to benefit all parties through sustained customer satisfaction.

2.8.3 Advantages of ISO 9000

ISO is an internationally recognised framework for Quality Management Systems. By employing the ISO standards, a better quality product is not guaranteed; it does increase the chances of a more satisfactory product being developed however. Kanholm (1999) states that the ISO 9000:2000 standards 'represent a more modern approach to quality management and is closer to current management system thinking'. Dawood (1994), stated of the ISO 9000:1994 standards that they were designed to create consistency and comprehensibility - by requiring documentation in both words and pictures.

Gillies (1992), supported by Casey (2000) states that there are two main reasons why software developers should seek ISO 9000 certification:

- The market-driven demand to achieve competitive advantage
- To set targets for a quality improvement programme

The ISO/TC 176 puts it more simply and says that an organization should implement ISO 9000 "To keep customers - and to keep them happy"! ISO/TC 176 says that ISO 9000 provides a framework that will consistently turn out products conforming to the customer's requirements - "And that means consistently happy customers" (ISO/TC176, 2003b).

2.8.4 Criticisms of ISO 9000

Gillies (1992) supported by Richardson (2000) states "The main difficulty experienced when applying ISO 9001 guidelines to software development is that the standard was not developed exclusively for software". In 1991, in response to this concern, ISO introduced 'ISO 9000-3: Guidelines for the application of ISO 9001 to the development, supply and maintenance of software', which was targeted at the IT community.

Companies seeking to retain or achieve ISO certification must be able to demonstrate continued improvement. However, when a company has been continually improving over a number of years, it becomes harder to show continued improvement. While most would argue that it is impossible to achieve perfection and that process improvement must be done on a continual basis, what happens when a company has achieved enough quality for their purposes? ISO does not recognise this business fact, and unless companies can demonstrate continual improvement, they will not get certification. 'ISO requires continual improvement. If there is no demonstrable improvement then the certifying body must withdraw registration' (Graham, 2002).

Another criticism levelled at earlier ISO standards were that they concentrated too heavily on documentation. Small companies in particular were cautious about investing in a model that they saw would tie up vital resources in documentation. However, the revised ISO standard ISO 9000:2000, requires only six processes to be documented in comparison to 18 processes in the 1994 standard (Liebesman, 2002). The standard introduces these new ideas and concepts with a ceratain lack of conviction, however. A typical example of this is for the identification of customer needs and expectations, it seems that the standard only introduces the new concepts without requiring proper structures to implement them (Kanholm, 1999).

2.9 ISO 15504

2.9.1 Introduction

The British Standards Institute (BSI) proposed that software process assessment be considered as an area for standardization and that a three part approach be used (SEI, 2002a):

1. A study period would be undertaken, followed by
2. The development of a draft international standard (Technical Report Type, resulting in
3. Registration as a full international standard.

Accordingly, in June 1991, a meeting of ISO/IEC JTC1/SC7 approved a study period (resolution 144) to investigate the needs and requirements for a standard for software process assessment (SPICE, 1998b). Following this in 1993 a project called Software Process Improvement and Capability determination was set up. This project is sometimes referred to as SPICE or as ISO 15504.

2.9.2 Software Process Assessment

In 1995 the draft standard for process assessment Version 1 was released. Version 2 was released in 1996 and the SPICE trials phase 2 started in parallel. The draft was later released as ISO/IEC TR15504 (Casey, 2000). These drafts formed the basis for a technical report entitled "Software Process Assessment" and consists of the following 9 parts (SPICE, 1998a):

1. Concepts and introductory guide
2. A model for process management
3. Rating processes
4. Guide to conducting assessment
5. Construction, selection and use of assessment instruments and tools
6. Qualification and training of assessors
7. Guide for use in process improvement
8. Guide for use in determining supplier process capability
9. Vocabulary

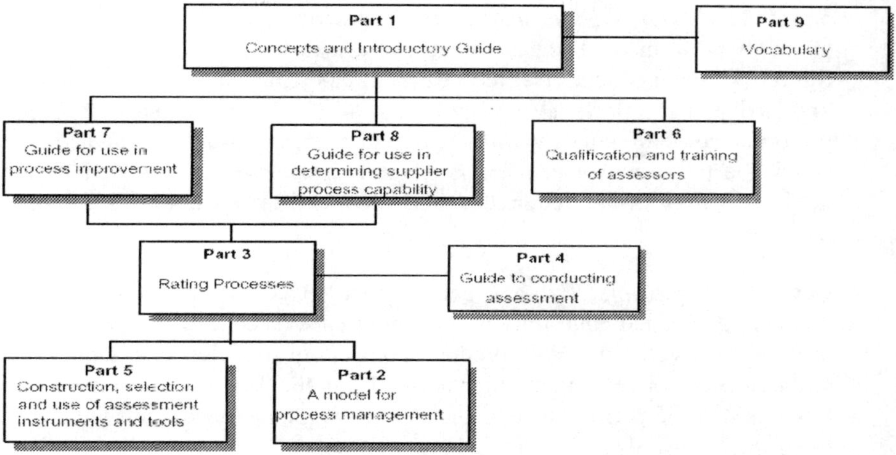

Figure 2.8. Components of SPICE (SPICE, 1998a)

2.9.3 Structure of SPICE

Process assessment examines the processes used by an organization to determine whether they are effective in achieving their goals (SPICE, 1998a). The SPICE framework includes architecture for rating practices and processes and for presenting assessment ratings. It is based on assessing a specific process instance. A process instance is a singular instantiation of a process that is uniquely identifiable and about which information can be gathered in a manner that provides repeatable ratings. Each process instance is characterized by a set of six process capability level ratings, each of which is an aggregation of the practice adequacy ratings that belong to that level.

Similar to the SW-CMM, SPICE contains capability levels, though SPICE has 6 levels compared to 5 capability levels in the SW-CMM. The SPICE architecture can be described as being two-dimensional – levels and processes (Magnani and Garra, 1998). SPICE differs from the SW-CMM in categorizing processes and capabilities by functional (single process instances) rather than organizational units (Gillies, 1997). The six levels are (SPICE, 1998b):

Level 0: *Not Performed:* There is general failure to perform the base practices in the process. There are no easily identifiable work products or outputs of the process.

Level 1: *Performed-Informally:* Base practices of the process are generally performed. The performance of these base practices may not be rigorously planned and tracked. Performance depends on individual knowledge and effort. Work products of the process testify to the performance. Individuals within the organization recognize that an action should be performed, and there is general agreement that this action is performed as and when required. There are identifiable work products for the process.

Level 2: *Planned-and-Tracked:* Performance of the base practices in the process is planned and tracked. Performance according to specified procedures is verified. Work products conform to specified standards and requirements. The primary distinction from the Performed-Informally Level is that the performance of the process is planned and managed and progressing towards a well-defined process

Level 3: *Well-Defined:* Base practices are performed according to a well-defined process using approved, tailored versions of standard, documented processes. The primary distinction from the Planned-and-Tracked Level is that the process of the Well-Defined Level is planned and managed using an organization-wide standard process.

Level 4: *Quantitatively Controlled:* Detailed measures of performance are collected and analyzed. This leads to a quantitative understanding of process capability and an improved ability to predict performance. Performance is objectively managed. The quality of work products is quantitatively known. The primary distinction from the Well-Defined Level is that the defined process is quantitatively understood and controlled.

Level 5: *Continuously-Improving:* Quantitative process effectiveness and efficiency goals (targets) for performance are established, based on the business goals of the organization. Continuous process improvement against these goals is enabled by quantitative feedback from performing the defined processes and from piloting innovative ideas and technologies.

Figure 2.9 below shows the relationship between process and levels. Note that processes can exist in more than one level, a concept that is alien to the Capability Maturity Model for Software, but similar to the continuous nature of the Capability Maturity Model Integration.

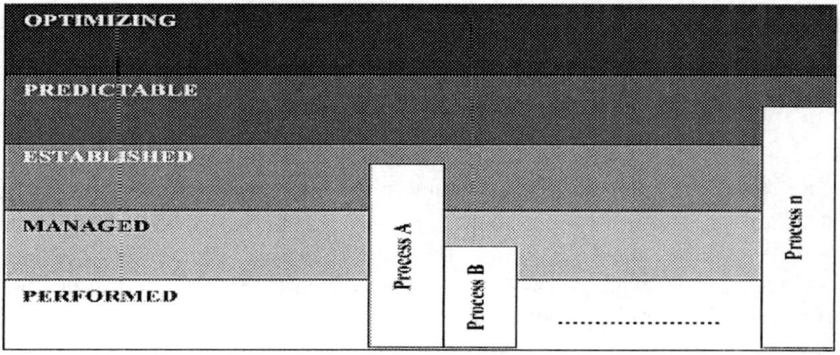

Figure 2.9. Relationship between Processes and Levels (Magnani and Garra, 1998)

SPICE is considered as being a continuous model for SPI. Part 7 of the SPICE standard states that change regarding the software process "is continuous - not a one-shot effort – it involves continual learning and evolution" (SPICE, 1998c). It is a cyclical model, where at a certain point processes and practices, having gone through the improvement model, are reviewed from step one again with a view to tweaking the process in some other way to provide added improvement.

2.9.4 Advantages of SPICE

Many of the principles used in SPICE are based on existing tried and tested models. SPICE gives credit for organisations with higher capability levels of individual processes as opposed to organisational wide capability. Another advantage of the SPICE framework is that it was designed not only for the large companies but the small ones as well. This means that smaller companies need not necessarily have to carry out extensive and time consuming tailoring on the framework used to implement it.

2.9.5 Criticisms of SPICE

SPICE is seen mainly as a European model for software process improvement and is not widely used elsewhere. As a result, organisation in other parts of the world may not be as familiar with SPICE, or as willing to accept the meaning of any certification in the model. This puts pressure on organisations - particularly the smaller ones who wish to do business outside of Europe - to ignore SPICE completely or to implement multiple models in order to satisfy multiple markets, which could prove more expensive and time consuming than the benefits received.

2.10 Other Methodologies

The software quality models, frameworks and standards discussed above are among the most popular currently used in software organisations throughout the world. However there are a variety of other development techniques and frameworks that are used. Some of these techniques and frameworks are briefly mentioned below.

2.10.1 Tick IT

Tick IT was initially developed by the British Standards Institute (BSI) as a guide for organizations seeking to implement the old ISO 9001-3 standard. There was reluctance among software organisations to implement the ISO standard; as a result Tick IT was developed. Though it is a standard in itself and certification can be independently achieved, it was originally viewed as going hand-in-hand with the ISO 9000 standard.

2.10.2 IT Infrastructure Library (ITIL)

ITIL is essentially a library of information to be used as an aid to implementing a framework for Information Technology service management. ITIL is aimed at those organisations that are providing an IT service, but not necessarily developing software. The ITIL Toolkit comprises five separate sections which act as a guide and aid to organisations seeking to implement the infrastructure library. ITIL was originally developed in the United Kingdom but its use is now worldwide.

2.10.3 Agile Software Development (ASD)

In a tutorial on Agile Methods, Scott Ambler describes Agile Software development as an approach to software development that is people-oriented, that enables people to respond effectively to change, and that results in the creation of working systems that meet the needs of its stakeholders (Ambler, 2004). There are a variety of different software development techniques that come under the Agile umbrella. These techniques include:

- Extreme Programming (XP)
- Scrum

- Dynamic System Development Method (DSDM)
- Feature Driven Development (FDD)
- Agile Modelling

2.11 Conclusion

The models, frameworks and standards discussed above are commonplace industry examples of software process improvement techniques. However there are weaknesses associated with each. Richardson (1999) argues that the models are very one-dimensional in their approach and that they do not take into account the potential knock-on effect that improvement techniques may have on other processes. She asks - "if the project software planning is coordinated, will this have an effect on other processes? Will this improve how the company deals with sub-contractors, for example? Or will it improve how the company carries out it's testing? It is also possible that practices will have a negative effect on some processes".

Software process assessment has been described as being "expensive, time consuming, exhaustive and disruptive to the organization being assessed" (Buchman and Bramble, 1995). And for the most part small companies with limited budgets and manpower cannot afford either the time or the money to spend on their process.

Just because an organization implements one of the models discussed above, it does not automatically mean that there will be an improvement in the product. The models are a part of the quality system that includes: management commitment, training and educating workers, setting and achieving goals for continuous improvement (Dawood, 1994). All are needed for a quality improvement programme to be a success.

The SW-CMM is an example of a staged model for software process improvement, while SPICE is an example of continuous software process improvement model. The strengths and weaknesses of each type of model are outlined below (see table 2.7.) (Magnani and Garra, 1998).

Table 2.7. Staged Vs Continuous

	Strengths	**Weaknesses**
Staged E.g. CMM	The organisation can implement an *improvement plan* aligned to one maturity level and its related key process areas.	*Rigid* approach with a predefined step-by-step implementation programme.
	The common features of each KPA represent a useful guide for the assessment activities and a simplified view for management.	Difficult to be *tailored*, e.g. for SME's.
Continuous E.g. SPICE	The organisation can define its *own improvement path*, selecting appropriate processes and defining an adequate capability profile for each of them.	There are no *pre-defined* improvement goals grouping processes and organisational and infrastructural issues.
	Easy to be *tailored* and *integrated* with other models.	The description of the base practices is made at a high level of *abstraction.*

The table below (table 2.9.) outlines the strengths and weaknesses of the SW-CMM, SPICE and the ISO 9000 models as adapted from Richardson (1999).

Table 2.8. Summary of Software Process Models adapted from Richardson, (1999)

Model	Strengths	Weaknesses
SW-CMM	• Improves software process • Specific set of guidelines	• Assessment is expensive • Lack of improvement model • Tailoring required for small companies • No credit for higher levels • One-dimensional
ISO 9000	• Market driven • Internationally recognised • Recognised outside software community • Improves software process • Reviewed every 5 years	• Lack of improvement model • One-dimensional • Extensive documentation required
SPICE	• Developed from existing models and experiences • Credit for higher levels • Specific set of guidelines	• Expensive assessment • Lack of improvement model • One-dimensional

Given the wealth of information that is available on process improvement models, the numerous models that are in existence at the moment, and the strengths and weaknesses of each; it is no easy decision for an organization to make regarding which model to implement. It cannot simply be a case of choosing the first model that comes to mind and hoping that it works out. Or even if it were to work out; who knows? - another model might have brought increased quality at a lesser price. A study to decide which process improvement model to implement is a project within itself and must be given the proper attention, so that the organization will select the model that is best suited to their organization.

However, given the recent rise of the CMMI, the researcher has concluded that it is a more "all-inclusive" software process model, at least on paper. It offers two representations of the model i.e. staged and continuous - and the benefits of both. It supplies extensive documentation on both representations. It is built upon the foundations of successful process models as devised previously. It provides the possibility of multiple dimensions of process improvement and can be tailored to the needs of small companies. Depending on the appraisal type you chose you could decide how expensive you want to make the appraisal process. Only time will tell whether the CMMI is the way forward; currently, it does appear to be ahead of its competitors, however.

Many factors must be considered by organisations that wish to implement a quality model. These factors include: cost, change required, ease of implementation, business goals, market requirements among others. The decision to implement a software process model within an organisation is not an easy one to make. However, with the right information, skills and resources organisations can successfully select and implement a software quality model that is suited to their particular organisation.

CHAPTER THREE

RESEARCH METHODOLOGY

3.1 Introduction

The overall aim of this research was to provide the Irish software community with the information required so as to better prepare them for competition on a global scale. The research presented in this volume can be divided into three separate sections. Firstly, research was conducted in India in collaboration with a large software-consulting organisation. This research examined the possible development of a methodology for the selection and use of software quality models within customer organisations. Secondly. research was carried out in Ireland to determine the attitudes of the Irish software community towards software quality. The experiences and use of software quality models in the Irish software industry was also examined. Finally, a comparison is made between the apparent focus on quality within the two countries software industries, as evidenced through their attitudes and experiences of software quality models. As a consequence of the unpredictable nature of research – (in general) - the intended focus of this research changed slightly over time. The changes in focus and the reasons for these changes will also be discussed in this chapter. Figure 3.1 below, provides a high-level flow-chart representation of the research methodology employed in this volume.

Both qualitative and quantitative research methods were used in gathering the data for this research. Examples of each research method used are presented and discussed along with methods and tools used to analyse data gathered from these research methods.

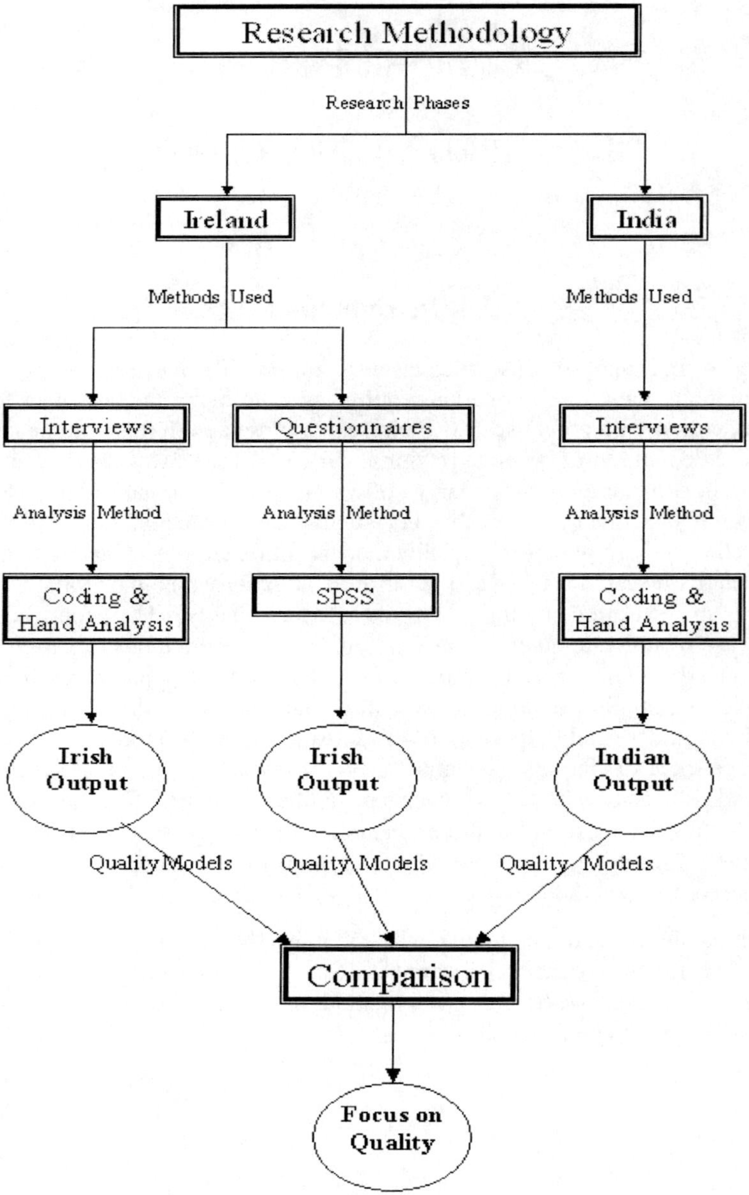

Figure 3.1. Flow-chart representation of the research methodology

3.2 Research Methods

3.2.1 Qualitative Research

Qualitative research methods are generally used to discover more about a particular topic or to gain a better insight into the subject area generally. The qualitative research as (primarily) employed during the course of this research, can be considered as a process of systematic inquiry into the meanings, which people employ to make sense of and guide their actions (McLeod, 1999). Qualitative research requires fuller and more flexible involvement by the researcher with those from or about-whom the data is being collected than is typical of other more quantitative approaches (Allen and Skinner, 1991). These methods provide the researcher the opportunity to ask complex questions and to prompt respondents in the right direction, should they stray from the point. They usually provide high quality data for the researcher to analyse. There are four major methods used by qualitative researchers:

- Observation
- Analysing tests and documents
- Interviews
- Recording and transcribing (Silverman, 1995)

Research interviews have been described as "a verbal interaction between one or more researchers and one or more respondents for the purpose of collecting valid and reliable data to answer particular research questions" (Parahoo, 1997). Interviews can place time and cost constraints on the researcher. It takes time not only to complete the interview but also to set up the interview. Depending on where the interviews are organised, travel costs may arise, usually on behalf of the interviewer, occasionally for the interviewee. Interviewees often have to give up valuable work time to participate in these interviews and would therefore not appreciate too much of their time being taken up with these matters. Interviews also offer little or no anonymity to the respondents and respondents may therefore be unwilling to discuss sensitive topics in detail. Interviewees may also feel under pressure to give answers that they feel the researcher wants to hear instead of what they actually believe. Another criticism of interviews as a research method is its subjectivity, and that "persons words can differ from their actions, and certainly the same word can mean different things to different people of in different situations" (Bailey, 1994). All of these points must be taken into account by the researcher when conducting the interviews and analysing the data received.

There are three main types of interviews: i.e. structured, semi-structured and unstructured. As a number of interviews would be conducted throughout the course of this research it was felt that a standardised approach would be the most suitable. Consequently, unstructured interviews were ruled out from an early stage since they offer little standardisation when conducting a large number of interviews. With structured and semi-structured interviews, the interviewer prepares a list of questions that they would like answered. Semi-structured interviews allow the interviewer to change the order of questions asked and to pursue a different line of questioning if it suits the situation. Structured interviews, on the other hand, do not allow as much flexibility – i.e. the questions are answered in order and interviewees are encouraged not to stray from the point by the interviewer. The researcher decided that semi-structured interviews would be the best type of interview to use since they offer standardisation - but with the option of flexibility – allowing follow-up and the pursuit of any train of thought that may emerge in an interview. Semi-structured interviews are used

> …To obtain a more intensive study of perceptions, attitudes, and motivations than a standardized questionnaire permits. This type of interview is useful in scouting a new area of research, to find out what the basic issues are, how people conceptualise the topic, what terminology people use, and what their level of understanding is (Judd et al., 1991)

As this research aimed to explore the attitudes, opinions and experiences of people towards a particular subject, it was felt that semi-structured interviews 'ticked the necessary boxes' when it came to a data collection methodology and this method was therefore used as the main research tool in both India and Ireland.

Two main types of questions can be asked in interviews – i.e. both closed and open-ended questions. Closed questions are designed in such a way that the answer would consist of a single word or a short phrase. They are intended to be quick and easy to answer. Quantitative researchers generally favour this type of question as the answers they produce lend themselves to simple tabulation (Silverman, 1995). An example of a closed question would be "how long have you worked for this company?". The intended answer for this question would be no longer than a few words e.g. "5 years". Open-ended questions are designed to get the interviewee to talk about the topic under review. The answers to open-ended questions are generally longer than those received from closed questions and need to be coded prior to analysis. They make the interviewee think about the answer they will provide and the author should (hopefully) receive the opinions and beliefs of the interviewee.

The method of recording the interviews used during this research involved both the use of digital voice recording equipment and note-taking. Note-taking is seen as a more informal method of recording interviews. The interviewee may be more likely to relax and open up this way - as opposed to when using voice recording equipment. One of the potential drawbacks of note-taking, however, is that there is the potential to miss some valuable piece of information the interviewee is providing, while the researcher is recording the notes. With this in mind, and when conducting an interview, the author minimised the note-taking aspect of the research. As soon as the interview was complete and still "fresh in the mind" of the author, the notes were written up and elaborated upon. A document was created for each interview conducted.

Voice recording equipment can be a very good aid to the interviewer. It allows the interviewer to concentrate fully on the interview and to worry about transcription later. This negates the possibility of missing vital information from the interviewee while taking notes. One drawback to this approach, however, is that sometimes interviewees may become less willing to answer sensitive questions when recording equipment is used. This can result in the data received not being of as good a quality as it could have been had the traditional note-taking approach been adopted. Voice recording equipment was used exclusively in Ireland by the author. The information from the voice recording equipment was then transcribed into individual documents for each individual interview.

In order to analyse the data contained in each document, these documents had to be "coded". From an early stage in this research, themes were identified for examination. These themes were then assigned codes. For example, interviewees were asked for their position within an organisation. Any time the interviewee referred to his/her position within an organisation the code "position" was attached to this section of the data. Any time the interviewee referred to customer complaints, the code "customer complaints" was attached to this section of the data. This process, called axial coding, allows the researcher to divide up the data and to reassemble it in new ways (Krueger, 1998). The complete list of codes used in this research can be found in Appendix C.

3.2.1.1 Tools Used

The software tool NVivo was used to aid the researcher in coding the interview documents. Using this tool, each individual document was examined in turn and individual codes were assigned to the relevant sections of each document. Relevant coded segments were then extracted taken from each interview document to form individual "coded" documents for each separate code. These "coded" documents contained only the information pertaining to the relevant code used.

Analysing qualitative data is a process of bringing order to masses of collected data … it is messy, ambiguous, time consuming, creative and fascinating process (Marshall and Rossman, 1989). Though interviews are essentially a qualitative research method, it is sometimes possible to identify certain statistical inferences from the answers given by interviewees depending on the information received. The coded documents were hand-analysed by the author to discover any emerging themes. For example, when analysing the coded "software development problems" document; the author identified and categorised "requirements problems" as an emerging and commonly occurring theme throughout the interviews. It was then possible to subsequently identify the number of times that requirements problems had occurred. This allowed the researcher to draw statistical inferences based on the qualitative data received. These and other statistical inferences were identified and categorised by the author and used to draw up results.

3.2.2 Quantitative research

Quantitative research refers to:

- The search for casual relationships conceptualised in terms of the interaction of variables, some of which (independent variables) are seen as the cause of other (dependent variables)
- The design and use of standardized research instruments (tests, attitude scales, questionnaires, observation schedules) to collect numerical data
- The manipulation of data using statistical techniques (Hammersley et al., 1994)

Quantitative methods are used to gather large amounts of data/ statistics about a particular topic or subject area. Examples of quantitative research methods include: questionnaires, either hard copy format (paper) or soft copy (online versions).

The questionnaire is a widely used and useful instrument for collecting survey information, providing structured, often numerical data. It can be administered without the presence of the researcher, and is often comparatively straightforward to analyse (Cohen et al., 2000). Questionnaires are a valuable medium for getting information, especially preliminary and background information in the research process (Davies & Preston, 2002). Advantages of using questionnaires, is that generally they provide quick results. The researcher has already specified a group of possible answers to each question, which allows better preparation for data analysis. Questionnaires are also more convenient for respondents as they are generally much quicker to complete than an interview. Questionnaires allow for a larger sample to be taken and allow respondents to the questionnaire a greater deal of anonymity, which may prove useful if sensitive topics are being discussed.

However, questionnaires are fixed in nature and allow the researcher no room to be flexible to adapt to something that may arise from its use. Questionnaires, particularly online versions, do not offer the researcher the opportunity to prompt the respondents if they are having trouble with a question. A further drawback is that respondents may only partially or incorrectly complete them. Questions tend to be short and to the point, restricting the ability of the researcher to pose complex questions.

Once collected, the data from a questionnaire can then be analysed and used to make statistical inferences about the surveyed population. However, before undertaking quantitative research of this nature a population for study needs to be identified. Factors such as expense, time and accessibility frequently prevent researchers from gaining information from the whole population. Therefore data is gathered from a smaller group or subset of the total population in such a way that it is representative of the total population under study (Cohen et al., 2000)

3.2.2.1 Tools Used

The information received from the questionnaire was analysed using the aid of a statistical analysis tool called SPSS. This allowed the researcher to produce graphical representations of data required to present research findings, as well as allowing for cross-comparison between questions. As such this was seen as a suitable tool for use when analysing the questionnaire data received.

3.3 Research in India

The author conducted research in India over a three-month period. The research was carried out in collaboration with an Indian owned software-consulting organisation and it's customers. A confidentiality agreement with the Indian organisation was made, and because of this the organisation cannot be named and will be referred to as AB Consulting (ABC).

ABC is one of the biggest consultancy firms in India employing approximately 45,000 people with a turnover of over $2 billion. It has offices throughout India including: Mumbai, Bangalore and Chennai. Their international offices are located around the world in countries including: United States of America, China, United Kingdom, Ireland and Hungary.

ABC offers services including information technology consulting and business process outsourcing. ABC is a branch of one of Asia's largest conglomerates. Their customers include: Boeing, Deutsche Bank, General Motors, IBM, Microsoft and Nokia. At the time of this research, ABC was CMM level 5 certified.

The concept behind the proposed research in India originated from ABC. It was their desire to develop "a methodology for enabling organizations to make a decision on the most suitable model/models for their software purposes". The outline for this research was presented in a concept note from ABC entitled "Customer Driven Process Benchmarking" (see Appendix D). ABC realised that customer organisations faced tough decisions when choosing to implement a software quality model. These decisions included but need not be limited to the following:

1. Which model to adopt?
2. How much to adopt (levels)?
3. What should be the timeline?

The concept note was discussed between the author and ABC. This was to ensure a full understanding by each party as to the research project. It was agreed that as a first step to developing the methodology, there was a need to identify why certain organisations chose to implement one particular quality model over another. Customers who had already implemented a quality model would have to be approached and asked for their input as well as the consultants that helped them make their decisions.

The input required from customers and consultants included information regarding the criteria that were used to select the chosen model. The reason as to why each specific criterion was used would also have to be examined. These criteria formed the basis of the decisions made as to which quality model to adopt and were therefore of vital importance to this research project.

What criteria were used to make the decision?

- What have customers and consultants done correctly?
- What have customers and consultants done incorrectly?

At this point, the author undertook to travel to India for a period of three months to work with ABC.

3.3.1 Understanding the Quality Process

3.3.1.1 Charter

The author, upon request from ABC, drew up a charter to give a high level informal overview of the project (see Appendix E). This charter discussed what needed to be done in order to collect the information required. The charter included possible criteria that might be focused on – (in detail) – so as to get the results needed. A possible set of interview questions were also presented so as to give the parties involved the opportunity to discuss these and refine them. It was decided to build and refine these interview questions and then to pilot the interview with the ABC consultants in order to obtain their feedback before rolling it out with other consultants and customers.

It was made clear to the author that there would be only one chance to elicit information from customers and that this opportunity would have to be as short and to-the-point as possible. It was understood that the more research conducted with consultants and customers, the more accurate the information received would be. It was eventually hoped to build up a database of customer information, which would continually be refined to produce more accurate results. A timescale was included in the charter to give a rough timescale of work required and how long this work would take.

3.3.1.2 Methodology Document

The charter was drawn up and discussed between the author and ABC. It was agreed that a more detailed view of the research project was required. With this in mind, the author drew up a "methodology document" (see Appendix F). This document detailed step by step what would be required to complete the research. Nine separate steps of the research project were identified that needed to be completed in order to come to a satisfactory end result. The steps involved and an explanation of each are presented in the table below (table 3.1.).

Table 3.1. Step by step through the Indian Research

Step	Explanation
1. Develop methodology document	Methodology document would be created to give a detailed plan of what work was to be done
2. Develop data collection plan (DCP)	DCP to determine how and who to interview. Interview questions developed and finalised
3. Pilot data collection plan within ABC	Pilot interviews to be conduced with ABC consultants
4. Data collection plan	Interviews to be conducted with larger groups of consultants
5. Analyse pilot data	Data received from both pilots to be analysed
6. Analyse information	All data received from the interviews to be coded and analysed. Data received from the customer questionnaire to be analysed

Each *step* of the methodology was divided into seven different *phases*:

1. Entry criteria – what must be done before work on the step can commence?
2. Tasks – identify each task that must be completed to finish each step
3. Verification – identify method of verifying step completion

4. Exit criteria – what has to be fulfilled for this step to be complete
5. Work products – what will be produced from this step
6. Effort required by ABC – identify effort that ABC will put into each step
7. Timeframe – identify the time required to complete each step

The verification phases required sign off from the ABC consultants dealing with the project before exit criteria could be met. The timeframe for the overall project was set between 15-17 weeks. Steps, 1-2 and 4-6 would be undertaken in India. ABC undertook to complete step 7 themselves. This would entail the author delivering a questionnaire to ABC. ABC employees would then use their personal relationships with customers to elicit the required information from them. The author would then complete steps 8 and 9 of this research in Ireland, once ABC had returned the data acquired from customers.

3.3.2 Research Methods Used

For the purpose of the research conducted in India it was decided to use both a qualitative and a quantitative method. A population for study needed to be identified. Consultants and customers were the logical choice of population. Consultants working in ABC have extensive knowledge in the field of quality models and software processes and as such were therefore identified as ideal candidates for interview. Customers are those facing the tough decisions. Though they may enlist the consultant to aid them in their decision it is ultimately the customer organisation that has to make it. As such, customers were identified as the logical choice for receiving questionnaires.

3.3.2.1 Interviews

The author interviewed the consultants in ABC, with the intention that they would add to the body of knowledge the researcher already had. It was hoped that through these interviews the author would gain a further insight into the practicalities of quality models in general and how they are selected. ABC consultants would also help to narrow the scope of the information required, in effect acting as a filter on behalf of the author.

The original charter (see Appendix E) that was written by the author contained a set of possible interview questions for the consultants. After further discussion with the ABC consultants who were involved in this research the interview questions were refined and finalised. The finalised set of interview questions used can be found in Appendix H. The interview was divided into 5 sets of questions. The first set contained introductory questions aimed at setting the interviewee at ease and giving the author a general background of the interviewee. The next set of questions related to quality model selection. The purpose of these questions was to gather as much information as possible from the consultant regarding what organisations consider when deciding which quality model to implement.

The third set of questions were concerned with quality model implementation. The author wanted to know about specific processes that may have been considered when deciding to implement a quality model. The aim was to attempt to identify what processes were considered problem processes prior to implementing a quality model and how and why this implementation affected the processes. In the fourth set of questions interviewees were asked about their personal opinions regarding processes, selection and implementation of quality models. The intention here was to get an informal view from the interviewee based on their personal experience with each. The fifth set, and final question asked if the interviewee wished to ask any questions or make any comments themselves

As the first set of questions were introductory and aimed simply at getting basic background information from the interviewee they were designed as "closed questions". The remaining questions were predominantly open-ended questions, as this was where the researcher wanted to elicit the more detailed information from the interviewee. An invitation to the interviewee to make any comments or ask any questions about the research was also included. This was designed to be "a gap filler". If any gaps were identified in the questions already asked, by making additional comments or by asking questions, the interviewee might highlight these gaps and allow the author to compensate for them.

The interview was semi-structured in nature. This method of interviewing allows for two-way communication between interviewer and interviewee. This method was deemed necessary to allow the researcher to pursue any train of thought that the interview may develop. It allowed for more discussion in the hopes of gathering more information. The original interview questions produced were reviewed and refined by ABC consultants working on this research project together with the author.

Once the questions were agreed upon, it was decided to pilot these questions with other ABC consultants.
Two initial interviews were conducted to allow the author to test the questions being used. Interviewees were given prior knowledge of the questions. The purpose of this was to give the interviewee advanced warning of what was to be asked and allow them to prepare for something they may potentially be unsure of. Interviewees were also given an explanation behind the research being conducted and were asked at the end of the interview to comment on the questions used. These interviews first and foremost provided the author with research data. Upon completion of the pilot, the author examined and further refined the interview questions until they are as they appear in Appendix H.

Once the pilot was complete and the interview questions refined, a further eight interviews were then carried out with a number of ABC consultants and customers. Similar to the pilot, interviewees were given the questions in advance as well as general information regarding the research being carried out. This time however they were not invited to comment on the questions being asked. Once the data from the interviews was collected, the researcher hand coded and hand analysed the data for emerging trends. The information received from this research is presented in a later chapter.

3.4 Emerging Trends

Interviews were also conducted with members of the Indian software community both consultants and clients. Following the study with the Indian software companies a high appreciation of quality; software processes and software quality models were emerging. Similar information regarding the Irish software industry was not currently available. Therefore the research expanded to explore the attitudes and experiences of members of the Irish software community towards quality in general and towards their use of software quality models.

Information was sought from members of the Irish software community that focused on their general attitude towards quality and their experiences of software processes. A personal definition of quality was sought from the individuals interviewed in addition to an enquiry as to what each interviewee perceived their company's definition of quality to be. Information regarding the interviewee's opinions and experiences of various software processes were sought. Attitudes and issues that were dealt with from customers were also examined. Research also focused on the perceived software development problems that Irish software organisations felt they experienced.

3.4.1 Comparison

Information gathered from the Indian phase of this research focused on the selection and use of software quality models. For informative and comparative purposes, the information sought from the Irish software industry focused on their experience, if any, with software quality models. The purpose was to discover:

- Are software quality models being used in the Irish software industry?
- Why software quality models are being used?
- Why would a model be evaluated but not implemented?
- Why do some organisations not implement any model?

3.5 Research in Ireland

Quality in Ireland had traditionally been only applied to the manufacturing industry. Given the now global economy and especially since the burst of the "dot com" bubble, the author wanted to explore how or if the Irish software community had catered for quality.

A "state of the nation" was proposed, whereby the author would conduct research into these attitudes and opinions and form conclusions based on the analysed data received. As this research was aimed towards discovering opinions and feelings towards a subject it was decided that interviews would be used as the primary research activity here. Interviews allow the researcher the opportunity to be flexible. It was felt that flexibility and one to one conversations with interviewees would best serve this research.

3.5.1 Research Methods Used

3.5.1.1 Interviews

The literature review section of this thesis discussed a paper by Garvin (1984) where he presented 5 different views on quality. These views were:

- Transcendental View
- User View

- Manufacturing View
- Product View
- Value Based View

As part of a separate project underway within the University of Limerick, interview questions were developed and designed based on these five variations or views of quality. Given that there can be a variety of different views of quality, this approach was intended to investigate the different opinions and attitudes of interviewees toward each perspective.

Similar to the interviews conducted in India, the interview questions used in the research in Ireland were comprised of both open ended and closed questions. Closed questions were used in the beginning of the interview, to gather general background information about the interviewee. It was hoped that these would provide the researcher with some useful information regarding the person being interviewed as well as setting the interviewee at ease for the upcoming open-ended questions. Open-ended questions were then used to gather the main body of data required from the interviewee. The list of interview questions used can be found in Appendix J. A total of 53 interviews were conducted and the data gathered was made available to the author. Two research assistants and an M.Sc. class in the University assisted the author in carrying out the interviews.

Personal contacts secured some interviews, while other companies upon being informed of the research were willing participants. A wide variety of personnel were interviewed ranging from CEO's to software engineers. This was seen important to the validity of the research. Through interviewing a range of employees across the management spectrum, it was hoped to gain as many perspectives as possible regarding quality in the Irish software community, not just the perspectives from the higher-ranking members of the organisation, but perspectives from those that are doing the groundwork.

Digital voice recording equipment was the main means of recording the interviews, while note taking was also used. Once the recorded interviews were complete and transcribed, they were returned to the author. This was a long process, but necessary in order to analyse the data received. For those employing the note taking technique, upon completion of the interview, notes were written up and elaborated on while still fresh in the mind of the interviewer.

One drawback noted during the transcription phase of the research was, as the author of this research was not the only interviewer, the author had no control of all interviews. It was found from an early stage that unfortunately, not all questions were being asked to interviewees. The author took this under consideration when analysing the information and developing conclusions.

In the results chapter of this thesis it can be noted that the word "respondents" often appears where one might expect to find the word "interviewee". This is to show that the author is aware that not every interviewee was asked or answered every question. Therefore, the results formed from particular questions or sets of questions were then based on the actual responses received to the questions and not from the overall response to the interviews.

3.5.1.2 Questionnaire

A researcher from Dublin City University (DCU) conducted an online questionnaire into quality model adoption rates in the Irish software industry. The data from this questionnaire was made available to the author for the purposes of this thesis. A total of 77 replies were received from the online questionnaire from 60 different companies.

The questionnaire provided a mix of qualitative and quantitative questions, allowing the respondent to click a box, or in some cases provide a few short words for an answer. Background information about the respondent's organisation was gathered. Data relating to organisations focus on quality, as well as data regarding experience with a variety of quality models was also gathered. The data collected from this online questionnaire was then made available to the author.
The raw data, without analysis, was provided to the author. This data was input into the statistical analysis software tool SPSS for analysis. Through the use of SPSS, frequency tables and cross tabulations were produced to aid the author in the analysis of this data. These results are presented in chapter relating to results found in Ireland.

A total of 16 questions were asked in the online questionnaire (see Appendix K). However not all of the questions were used by the author in this research. Questions most relevant to the author's research were identified. These questions then became the focus of the author's analysis of the data received from the online questionnaire.

3.6 Conclusion

In this chapter the two main research methods qualitative and quantitative are discussed. Examples are given for each and their merits and drawbacks are examined. The research conducted was divided into two separate areas, the research in India and the research in Ireland. The Indian research methodology focuses on the development of a methodology document that eventually led to a formalised process document for the purposes of this research project. The research methods used in India, how they were developed and analysed are also discussed. An introduction to the research in Ireland is given. Research methods employed in the Irish phase of this research are discussed, including their design, use and tools used to analyse the data received.

CHAPTER FOUR

INDIAN ATTITUDES TO SOFTWARE QUALITY

4.1 Indian Software Industry

4.1.1 Overview

In 1999, India's software industry employed an estimated 200,000 people and was one of the fastest growing sectors of the economy. Annual industry revenues for 1999 were predicted to be around $4 billion, of which $2.7 billion was from software exports (Bagchi, 1999). However, due to the increase in global outsourcing and the initial successes from India, the market capitalization of Indian software companies skyrocketed from $4 billion in 1999 to $55 billion in June 2000 (Moitra, 2001). Computer software and Information Technology Enabled Services (ITES) exports is estimated at $17.2 billion for the year 2004-2005. This figure is an increase of 34% from $12.8 billion for the previous year (DIT, 2005).

Currently, the outsourcing industry in India is estimated to employ 1 million people (Ribeiro, 2005). At current rates, there will be approximately 17 million people available to the IT industry in India by 2008 (Accenture, 2004). With a large labour pool and favourable labour costs, India continues to be the world's leading exporter of software services (Krishnadas, 2005). The country's share of the lucrative global IT services market is estimated to be worth more than $350 billion for the year 2002-2003, representing a 1.9% increase on the previous year (Bharati, 2005). In 2001, India's share of the global markets for offshore IT and IT-enabled services were estimated at 25%, second only to Ireland. For offshore IT-enabled services only the figure was estimated at 67%. India has done more than just emerge as one of the top nations when it comes to global software development and IT services, India is now the nation to which all others must compete with and measure themselves against.

The success of the Indian software industry is not in spite of the global economic downturn, it is in part because of it. Organisations from around the globe are looking to cut costs and save money. Indian software companies provide an attractive cheaper alternate than other indigenous companies. It is not only in the software exports and outsourcing areas that the Indian software industry is growing. The Indian domestic software market managed a momentum of around 13% between 2002-2003 (Accenture, 2004).

4.1.2 Reasons for growth

What has made India such an attractive option for large multi-national corporations? According to a report published in 2001, there are five factors, which have contributed to the Indian success story:

- Availability of a highly competent and large talent pool
- World-class quality and high process maturity
- Competitive cost structures
- Rapid delivery capability
- No language barrier (English-speaking resource pool) (Moitra, 2001)

The Indian government's Department of Information Technology (DIT) attribute the IT sector's sustained success to:

> "Strong fundamentals comprising a large and growing pool of qualified, English speaking manpower, keen focus on defining and adhering to global quality standards, the demonstrated emphasis on information security, the improving levels and strong government support – focused on improving basic infrastructure and developing policies and an effective regulatory regime that favour the growth of the industry" (DIT, 2005)

Quality is one of the major concerns for many industries considering offshore outsourcing. However this has become a selling point for the Indian software houses (McLaughlin, 2003). According to the United Nations Conference on Trade and Development (2004), "India has earned a strong reputation on account of high quality services and IT firms in India typically hold the necessary quality certifications". Large inflows of Foreign Direct Investment (FDI) have also helped the Indian software industry grow. Though India may not have the infrastructure required for heavy (hard) industry, soft industries like IT services need no roads or railways to cross. A simple e-mail is all it takes to transfer code or programs from one place to another.

4.1.3 Challenges facing the Indian Software Industry

Indian software companies can outdo their European rivals with low wage costs and outclass them with a higher focus on quality. So what does the Indian software industry have to worry about? Several challenges face the Indian software industry. Among these challenges are:

- Political opposition to outsourcing
- Competition from China
- Growth in wage costs
- Domestic software industry

Political opposition to outsourcing is growing, especially within the United States. This is a genuine concern for the Indian software industry. So much so that the Indian National Association of Software and Service Companies (NASSCOM) have hired a New York based public relations firm to promote offshore outsourcing and lobby against legislation being introduced to curtail it (McLaughlin, 2003).

More than $1 billion in foreign direct investment arrives in China each week. By 2008 China will be the world's third largest exporter, and by the decade's end it's economy will be larger than that of either France or the United Kingdom (Pitsilis, Woetzel et al., 2004). In 2003, China received $53 billion in foreign direct investment, or 8.2% of the world's total – more than any one country (Farrell, Khanna et al., 2004). Though this seems like a large amount of FDI for China, it is low relative to its GDP. A large pool of skilled people and low costs are China's key advantages, but language skills and cultural factors tend to tilt the scales against China and in favour of India (UNCTAD, 2004).

According to a 2004 article in the Chief Information Officer (CIO) magazine, wage costs in the IT service industry in India rose by 14% (Overby, 2004). The wage costs still remain low when compared to US or European alternatives. Should wage costs continue to rise, organisations seeking to outsource will have to consider alternatives. With China still developing it's own markets, infrastructure and software industry they may soon develop enough to be a serious competitor to India's outsourcing magnates.

India's domestic software industry has grown over the past number of years but at a slow pace. According to a NASSCOM report, the domestic software and services sector was worth approximately $3.9 billion from

2003-2004, an increase of $0.9 billion from the previous year. Despite this increase, the domestic software market in India is growing at a marginal rate, especially when compared to the software and service exports (NASSCOM, 2005). The slow performance of the domestic software and services market could develop into a serious problem for the Indian software industry. At the moment, India is over-reliant on its export-oriented market. Should the challenges facing India's dominance of the outsourcing market continue, this over-reliance could become a serious problem.

4.2 Research in India

India's IT companies have recognised the need to show potential foreign investors the capabilities and maturity of their processes. It may not be a 'sure thing', but certification or accreditation with quality models or standards can show potential clients that Indian software companies have what it takes to deliver quality products. Many internationally recognised quality models, frameworks and standards currently exist. All of these models if used correctly can offer notable gains to organisations willing to spend the time and effort to implement them. However, choosing the right model to implement is not easy and a variety of factors must be considered. Once a model has been selected, further considerations include: how much of the model to implement, how to implement the model and whether or not to pursue accreditation or certification in the model.

4.2.1 Research Findings

From our initial meetings with software consultants, it was evident that for software development organisations there is a clear business need to demonstrate mature software processes. This need does not arise exclusively from any internal pressure to improve processes or services, but the external pressure to stay alive in a competitive market place. These organisations must implement a quality model or framework, and more often that not the model chosen is dictated by one of two things – either a direct customer requirement or the requirements of the market place.

The research then focused on software development departments within organisations whose main business was not software, but have significant IT departments. Interviews were carried out with customers who have implemented various models such as those mentioned earlier. The software consultants who advise such organisations on their software process were also interviewed.

4.2.1.1 What prompts change?

When the research was carried out with Indian companies, it was evident that the three major factors influencing change were:

- Competitive advantage
- Profit
- Customer complaints

Competitive Advantage
There exists a competitive advantage for organisations that can show that they are certified or have achieved a given CMM level. Prospective customers see the ability to demonstrate mature processes reflected by certification or maturity level as an influencing factor in selecting to whom they should give their business. The higher a maturity level an organisation has, the better chance they have of obtaining a valued customer contract.

It was also evident that a business goal of breaking into a new market dominated by organisations with specific certification or maturity levels was an influencing factor. Organisations stood a better chance of competing if they could at least match up to their competitors' demonstrated quality processes.

A direct customer request for the organisation to have a particular model implemented at a specific level was a common factor in the decision to implement an SPI model.

Profit
Everyone from top level management to quality consultants that were spoken to said that the desire to improve the "bottom line" was seen to be a major influencing factor in the decision to implement a quality model. Organisations do not implement a quality model just for the sake of it, they do it because they see the financial benefits. Whether the desired goal is improved project scheduling, reduction in costs, increase in productivity, higher rate of return on investment, all play their part in convincing management of the need to implement some form of a quality model.

Customer Complaints
The third major factor influencing the way an organisation's processes work, was customer complaints or production problems. When either of these has been traced back to the IT division, ultimately leading to loss of business, a quality model project was implemented. In an increasingly demanding market place, there is a need for the IT division to be leaner, meaner and more agile in order to meet the business demands not only of its external customers, but also of its internal customers who rely upon them for product support and maintenance.

The incentive of improved process performance was not found to be the primary goal of implementing any SPI strategy. One quality manager said "actual process improvement was not considered relevant during the implementation process and the fact that it was noted after implementation was considered an added bonus"!

4.2.1.2 Why choose one model over another?

Organizations must be very careful when considering the daunting number of quality models and frameworks, as the field is truly a quagmire in which process improvement efforts can be bogged down (Sheard, 1997). In deciding which quality model to implement top level management must clearly understand what it is they want to change and why they want to change it. There must be a clear understanding of the core business needs and goals of the organisation. Casey and Richardson (2002) state that "without a clear understanding of why an improvement initiative is undertaken, it will in most circumstances be doomed to failure, given the level of commitment required by all concerned for its successful conclusion"

From the research carried out in India, it was discovered that the main reasons given as to why certain models were considered for selection, but not actually implemented were:

- There was no tangible benefit for implementing the model
- Practices were implemented just to satisfy the model and not for business reasons.

Tangible Benefit
Managers need to be convinced of the value of process improvement. Process improvement takes time to institutionalise and requires a commitment from management in order to succeed (King, 2002). During

this research it was evident that for management to be fully committed to any SPI initiative, they require clear and tangible benefits (return on investment) that a particular quality model would bring their organisation before deciding whether or not to implement. One senior manager with responsibility for project and quality management asks "*Does implementing this model bring substantial benefit?*". If this question cannot be satisfactorily answered, then the model will not be pursued.

> "When push comes to shove, what really matters to management are the numbers" and the answers to questions such as: will this investment save us money? and what is the projected payback period and return on investment?" (Reifer, 2002).

Business Goals

In choosing a particular quality model over another the organisation needs to ensure that the model can fulfil most if not all of the organisation's primary business goals. "Your objective is not simply to satisfy the model's expectations" (Wiegers, 1999), but to ensure that your organisation's expectations are satisfied by the model. Our evidence suggests that with this in mind, organisations must ensure that there is a clear business reason for each practice or key process area being implemented and that practices are not being implemented to satisfy a particular model. One interviewee states that models under consideration "*must be in line with the strategic objectives of the company*".

4.2.1.3 What needs to be considered?

Interviewees were asked, "What needs to be considered by an organisation that has chosen to implement a software quality model?" From this research it was clear that there are several factors that need to be considered. These include:

- What change is required?
- Where and how to start?
- What is the timeframe and budget?

Change Required

According to one interviewee "*Implementation brings change, the organisation needs to assess its own ability to manage this change*" before implementing a quality model. The ease of which such a change can be implemented is a major factor that organisations must consider. The size of an organisation, the current state of the process and practices as well as how the organisation has been performing over the last number of years affect how easy the implementation process would be and how much change is required within the organisation. According to one senior quality consultant "*organisations size of course plays an important role as well as the current strength of the organisation's processes*". The organisation must be prepared to ensure that a high level of change does not result in failed implementation. This necessitates having the right people in the right place with enough knowledge and expertise to carry out the implementation process.

Where and how to start

Organisations must not aim too high too fast as disillusionment may set in. Some of the organisations seen during this research have chosen to start off small, implementing improvements on a set of processes or projects, noting the results and subsequently rolling out the model on an organisation wide basis. One interviewee suggests a gradual approach, "*If the change is gradual and there is visible improvement, workers may begin to understand and accept the changes*". Weigers (1999) advocates this approach, advising organisations to "select a small set of appropriate practices that will address your current process shortcomings and move toward your goals. Identify a project or two on which to pilot new processes and make adjustments before officially rolling them out". This has the effect of showing both management and staff the benefits of such improvements and keeping them fully focused and committed on continued improvement throughout the organisation. Process improvement is a continually improving cycle, not a static achievable plateau.

Timeframe and budget

Our investigation within Indian companies, leads to a warning for management. They must set both a realistic timeframe for the implementation as well as a realistic budget. Several interviewees state that the "budget and timeframe" allocated to the implementation of a quality model "must be realistic". The desire to improve must not result in situations where process improvements are rushed to meet unrealistic deadlines, as this could lead to the people involved doing what they are doing without knowing why they are doing it. It must be determined if external certification/ assessment is required, how the organisation would get certified/ assessed and how much this would cost. Management must appreciate that sometimes software process improvement initiatives may be costly, but in time if managed correctly they will pay for themselves.

4.3 Conclusion

For software organisations in India there was no choice in implementing a software quality model. Either a quality model was implemented or business would dry up. The choice for these organisations was which model to implement. Usually this decision depended on market forces or a customer requirement. Research then focused on the selection and use of software quality model in non-software organisations with signification software of IT departments.

The research first looked at what influences an organisation to decide to implement a quality model. Three major factors influencing change within these organisations were identified. These factors were: competitive advantage, improved bottom lines and customer complaints. An interesting fact noted here was that actual process improvement was not considered as an influencing factor in the decision to implement a quality model.

Once the decision to implement a quality model has been decided and a suitable model selected, the organisation must consider several factors. The amount change required by the organisation and how this change is managed could make or break any implementation attempt. Organisations must decide where and how exactly to commence the implementation of the model, and management within the organisation must be prepared to set a realistic budget and timeframe for the implementation.

The author has concluded from the Indian phase of this research that Indian software organisations have widely accepted the use of software quality models. This is primarily reflected in Indian software organisation's belief that there is a necessity to have a software quality model in place in order to stay in business. This research shows that Indian software organisations give great consideration to the selection and implementation process of a software quality model. All things considered this gives Indian software organisations a valuable bargaining chip when it comes to attracting foreign investment.

CHAPTER FIVE

IRISH ATTITUDES TO SOFTWARE QUALITY

5.1 Irish Software Industry

5.1.1 Overview

In a report compiled by the Central Statistics Office (CSO) of Ireland in 2004 on behalf of the sitting Irish government it was reported that the Information and Communication Technology (ICT) sector in Ireland in 2002 employed 82,100 people. Turnover for the sector was reported at €49 billion, equivalent to 17% of total value added in industry and services. When further divided the "computer and related activities" sub-section accounted for 22,211 employed and a turnover of €6.6 billion. The largest contributor to both employment and turnover was the ICT Manufacturing sub-section, which accounted for 33,488 employed and a turnover of €29.4 billion annually. This included the manufacturing of computers and household electrical appliances (Central Statistics Office, 2004). Focusing exclusively on the software industry in Ireland, it is estimated that 23,930 people were employed in 2003, a drop of 14% from the previous year. Revenue for the industry in 2003 was estimated around €14.9 billion, a 7% increase on the previous year (NSD, 2004)

According to ICT Ireland the ICT sector employs almost 90,700 people in over 1,300 companies up from 19,000 in 1990 (ICT_Ireland, 2005b) with a turnover of €52 billion in 2003 (ICT_Ireland, 2005a). The Irish Software Association (ISA) agrees with these estimates in its annual review of 2004, stating that in the last 25 years, "several thousand companies have been created along with 30,000 indigenous jobs – 90,000 when we factor in the multinational jobs" (ISA, 2004).

Although it employs less than 2% of the total workforce, the sector generates revenues equivalent to more than one tenth of Irish Gross Domestic Product (GDP) (HotOrigin, 2002). An Accenture report commissioned by ICT Ireland agrees with this "As well as contributing to job creation and export growth the sector is also a major contributor to the exchequer". The report went on to say that the ICT sector in Ireland is dominated by foreign owned Multinationals who contribute almost 70% of the jobs in the sector overall. However indigenous companies dominate the eBusiness and Enterprise Application Integration Software Sectors (Accenture, 2004).

The figures presented above from the various organisations and institutions vary to a degree. However all of these statistics highlight the continued importance of the ICT sector and with it the Irish software industry to the Irish economy.

5.1.2 Recovery of the Celtic Tiger

Since the downturn in the global economy, the Celtic tiger economy of Ireland has suffered, though signs of a recovery are evident. According to the European Information Technology Observatory in 2004 the Global ICT market will grow by 4.3% from 2,071 billion to 2,160 billion and in 2005 the market is predicted to grow by 6% to 2,291 billion (Accenture, 2004). Some Irish colleges are seeing this recovery with an increase in the number of school leavers applying for IT related degree courses. The following table (see table 5.1) drawn up from statistics from the Central Applications Office (CAO) of Ireland shows the total number of first preference applications for the Engineering/ Technology area. This is then separated into applicants to degree courses and diploma/ certificate courses.

The overall picture still suggests a degree of uncertainty in the ICT sector. The total number of first preference applications for the Engineering/ Technology area is at its lowest point over the period 1999-2003 is still 7600 under its peak period of 1999. As can be seen from the above tables, first preference university applications in the Engineering/ Technology area peaked in the year 2000 with 9,743 applications. Applications now appear to be on the increase at least for degree courses. However applications for diploma/ certificate courses are at its lowest number over the five-year period.

Table 5.1. First Preference Applications to IT related courses

First Preference Applications (Total List) *Engineering/ Technology*				
1999	*2000*	*2001*	*2002*	*2003*
26988	25942	24494	19931	19352

Degree List					**Diploma / Certificate List**				
1999	*2000*	*2001*	*2002*	*2003*	*1999*	*2000*	*2001*	*2002*	*2003*
9515	9743	9460	7815	8375	17473	16199	15034	12116	10977

(CAO, 2003)

Third level institution's degree courses are not the only ones suggesting a recovery. The Small Firms Association (SFA) of Ireland sees signs of recovery in the Celtic Tiger. In their 11th annual report on employment in Ireland the SFA project that small businesses in Ireland will create up to 61,003 new jobs in 2005, up from 36,283 new jobs created in 2004. Pat Delaney, director of the Small Firms Association says; "for the first time in our history Ireland will have 2 million people at work". Delaney goes on to give a message to the Irish government "a low taxation, low interest, low inflation environment leads to economic expansion and job creation" (SFA, 2005).

5.1.3 Reasons for Success

Ireland and its software community have enjoyed the benefits of lucrative outsourcing and investment from large Multi National Corporations (MNC's) especially from the United States of America. The reason for Ireland's economic success over the past decade has been attributed to several factors, which can be divided into ICT specific, and Non-ICT specific factors:

ICT Specific Factors

- Growth in global trade and the expansion of the US economy
- Growth foreign direct investment globally in the 1990s
- Education and technological innovation
- Upgrading of Ireland's telecommunications infrastructure

Non-ICT Specific Factors

- The enhancement of the enterprise environment created by reform of the public finances, reductions in taxation and wage moderation under the national partnership agreements
- Demographic trends that ensured that labour supply did not limit growth potential
- Deployment of EU structural and cohesion funds to Ireland
- English speaking workforce

(Enterprise Ireland, 2004; Forfas, 2004; Trauth, 2000).

5.1.4 Worldwide Investment

In the 2004 World Investment Report (WIR) from the United Nations Conference on Trade and Development (UNCTAD) it was found that economies such as the Czech Republic, Hong Kong (China) and Ireland continued to attract significant investment even during the Foreign Direct Investment (FDI) recession. In 2003 China overcame the United States of America as the largest receiver of FDI (UNCTAD, 2004).

In 2001, Ireland, India, Canada and Israel, in that order, accounted for over 70% of the total market for offshored services, mostly in software development and other IT-enabled services estimated to have been $32 billion, with Ireland accounting for one quarter of this. Among developing countries India is the preferred destination of offshore IT services as they boast "low cost skilled labour with first-mover and agglomeration advantages" (UNCTAD, 2004).

5.1.5 Concerns

The influx of new members to the European Union (EU) coupled with Ireland's recent status as one of the richer EU nations has resulted in the reduction of valuable EU grants. Since the "dot com" bubble burst there has been a large downturn in the number of school goers pursuing college degrees with a technological background, resulting in the possibility of labour shortages in the ICT sector in the short-medium term future.

The Expert Group on Future Skills Needs (EGFSN) warn that "the ICT sector downturn (since 2000) has caused an excess of supply over demand for graduates, but the expected recovery in demand may lead to a shortage of graduates in the medium-term". They go on to say that "Supply and demand are reasonably well balanced for computing degree graduates up to 2006. Thereafter, the analysis shows that demand is likely to overtake supply, and eventually exceed it by a substantial margin" (EGFSN, 2003).

The emergence of developing nations such as India and China as major players on the world's technological stage has given the Irish software community cause for concern. These nations and others like them can provide an ever-increasing, well-educated workforce for their ICT sector but more significantly can deliver this workforce at a much lower cost. There also appears to be a higher focus on quality particularly within Indian organisations as they seek to out do their own domestic, continental and western competitors in their bid to secure lucrative foreign investment deals.

So, given the worldwide burst of the "dot com" bubble, the recognised slowdown in the world's leading economies as well as the stumbling, but recovering Celtic Tiger Economy of Ireland over the past number of years, is there anything that can be done to help the Irish software community in their fight to keep jobs and retain and expand profits?

5.1.6 Potential Solutions

The Irish government must lead by example. Ireland's low cost corporation tax (at 12.5%) is a huge incentive for foreign companies looking to set up base in Europe. According to Cathy Phillips, editor of the Tax Notes International journal, "With one of the lowest corporate tax rates in the European Union (EU), Ireland has seen its economic growth consistently outpace that of its neighbours" (Phillips, 2005). The Government has delivered a number of world-class eGovernment projects for example Revenue Service On-Line (ROS), Office of Civil Service and Local Appointments Commissioners (OSLAC), Land Registry. However more can and should be done to exploit the potential of Information Technology to deliver enhanced services at a reduced cost (Accenture, 2004).

The projected shortfall in skilled graduates may eventually be overturned with time as confidence returns to the sector. In the mean time, this shortfall could be made up by an influx of skilled foreign workers. Pay cuts or pay freezes do not seem plausible in a country where the cost of living is already one of the highest in Europe. It is also unlikely that even with severe pay cuts the wage costs be unable to rival that of a developing economy.

One possibility is for the Irish software community to embrace the desire to improve the quality of their process and therefore the quality of their products in the way that Indian companies appear to have. If the Irish software community could do this and be able to demonstrate mature, capable and traceable processes it could prove the decisive factor for attracting untapped foreign investment potential and retaining existing foreign investment.

With this in mind it was decided to conduct research within the Irish software industry. The intention of this research was to gauge the general attitude towards quality within the Irish software community. Opinions on quality, customer attitudes towards processes and organisations' experiences with processes and software development were sought. Data was collected via interviews and questionnaires.

5.2 Research Findings

5.2.1 Interviewee Background

The aim of this research was to gauge attitudes and opinions towards software quality within the Irish software community, not just the opinions of the Chief Executive Officers (CEO's) but from all levels of the organisation. Of the 53 interviews conducted, 40 interviewees or 75% of total interviewed gave an answer as to what position they held within the organisation. The chart below (Figure 5.1.) shows the breakdown of the level of positions held by the interviewees.

It was found that out of these 40 respondents, 7 of those (17.5%) were in the top-tier of management at CEO/ Owner level. Five (12.5%) of those were mid-level management being directors, vice-presidents or senior managers. Thirteen (32.5%) of respondents were low-level management holding managerial positions such as quality or product managers. Nine respondents (22.5%) held senior positions within a team consisting of senior developers/ engineers, senior analysts or systems architects. The remaining 6 (15%) respondents held lower level staff positions such as engineers and developers

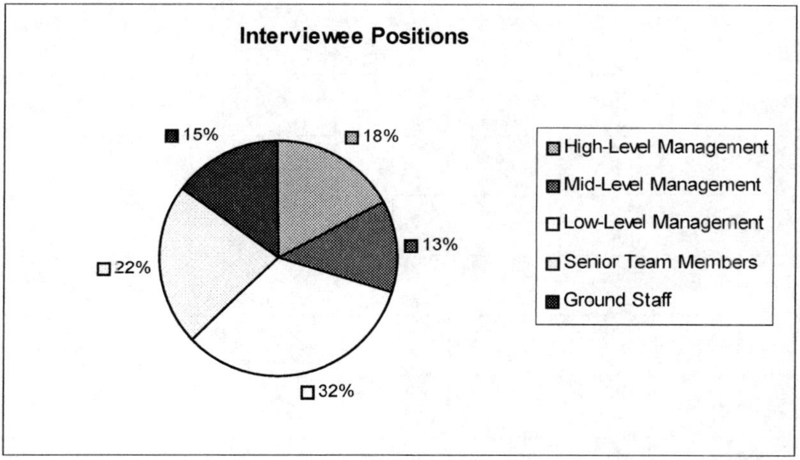

Figure 5.1. Interviewee Positions

Many of those interviewed were employed in small to medium sized enterprises (SME's). Due to the nature of such enterprises, many employees from across the management spectrum regularly wear hold multiple positions at once. On one hand an interviewee may have been the CEO or a Vice-President, dealing with important customer and sales issues as well as long term strategic planning for the organisation. The same person may also have been responsible for simple design and development issues that arise on day-to-day basis within the organisation.

5.2.2 Qualification Background

From analysing the research data, it was found that of the 40 interviewees that made their position within the company known, 30 provided information as to their qualification background. Of these 30, only one had no formal qualification from a third level institution but had 10 years industry experience, while another had a 'City and Guilds' academic qualification with 20 years industry experience. That leaves 29 respondents (97%) that have a formal third level qualification (including the City and Guilds). The table below (table 5.2.) shows the breakdown of qualification areas of the 30 respondents.

Table 5.2. Qualification background of interviewees

Job Type / Qualification	*Top-Level*	*Mid-Level*	*Low-Level*	*Team Leads*	*Team Members*	*Totals*
Computers	3	2	2		6	13
Business/ Commerce	2		4			6
Engineering		1	1	3		5
Maths	1	1				2
Management				1		1
Science			1			1
City and Guilds			1			1
No Qualification				1		1
Totals	6	4	9	5	6	30

What is more important though, is that there appears to be a desire to continue learning. Of the 29 respondents that had a qualification from a third level institution, 15 (51%) had completed further education either via postgraduate courses or other work related training courses. It is not clear however if this desire to continue learning is a personal ambition of the individual or if it is driven by the organisations seeking to further train their employees. Either way it reflects positively on the Irish software community.

5.2.3 Personal Quality Definitions

Interviewees were asked two separate questions regarding their opinions on quality in general and software quality. For the purpose of this research these answers were combined in order to give a more complete impression of their overall views of quality. From the information received from the 46 interviewees that answered this question it was evident that personal quality definitions centred around 4 main areas; customer oriented, ability to meet requirements, reliability/ efficiency and process oriented. The pie chart below shows the breakdown of personal quality definitions received.

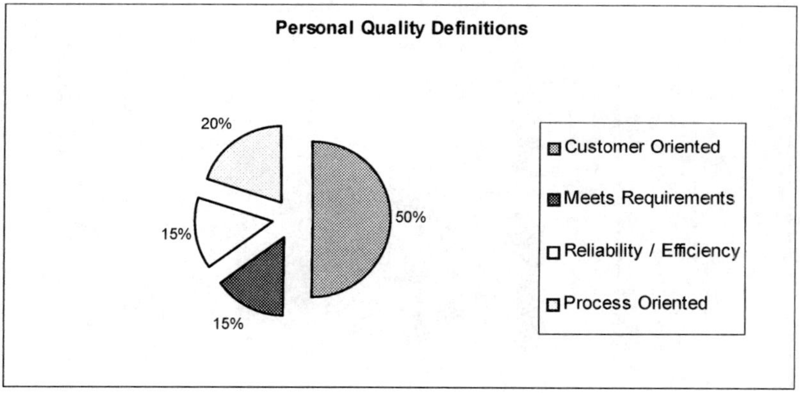

Figure 5.2. Breakdown of Personal Quality Definitions

As can be seen from the chart above, the majority of personal quality and software quality definitions received have been in the nature of pleasing customers. The following list summarises the percentage of definitions received:

- A system that satisfies the customers needs – 50%
- Getting the process or the build up to a product right – 20%
- Meeting the requirements set out for the product – 15%
- Reliability of the product and performance based on cost – 15%

An interesting question arises from this data. What exactly does 'pleasing a customer' or 'satisfying a customer' mean?

The interviewees have offered varying opinions regarding this. These opinions centre around three areas:

- Meeting the requirements or needs of the customer
- How the product performs for the customer
- Ensuring the customer gets value for money

As can be seen from the bar chart below (Figure 5.3.), the majority of respondents believe the key to satisfying customers lies in their ability to meet customer requirements. Seven believed that performance related issues were important to satisfying their customers, while 5 said that giving the customers a product relative to what they are willing to pay was central to satisfying them.

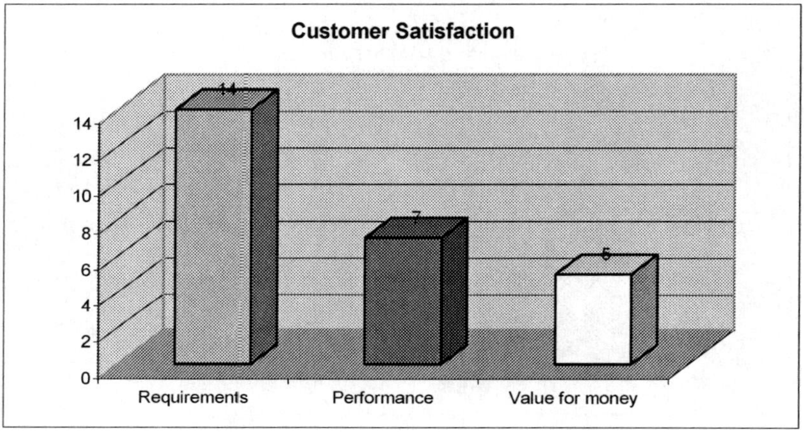

Figure 5.3. How to Satisfy Customers: Personal

One interviewee however gave an answer that the researcher found difficult to categorise. When asked to give a personal definition of quality, the interviewee responded saying "*the ability to get the job done to the customer's satisfaction*". This statement is clearly customer centred. It cannot be drawn from this definition how to satisfy a customer. This definition says a lot, not in terns of what has been stated, but by what has been left unsaid. A customer may be an individual or a global organisation each with it's own ideas on what they want, how they want it and how much they are willing to pay for it. It is each individual user of a product that determines what a good quality product is for them. In order to satisfy either an individual customer or a customer base, one must first know the customer, know what they need and how much they are willing to pay for it.

Without specifying what it is to satisfy a customer, this respondent has raised an interesting question. How can an unknown customer be satisfied? This seems a difficult prospect. Never the less, 96% of respondents were able to do so and the bar chart presents the breakdown of their opinions regarding what constitutes customer satisfaction.

5.2.4 Company Quality Definitions

When the interviewees were asked what was their company's definition of quality and software quality, some were unable to comment as they were not aware of any formal statement their company had on quality issues. This might be expected of a new recruit to an organisation to be unaware of any quality statement or focus on quality. However, interviewees were often senior developers or technical heads of departments. The response to this question was often "I do not know" or "I am not aware of any formal definition". Having a quality statement or definition for a company does not necessarily mean that they regularly produce quality products or have a high focus on quality. But in not having a quality statement and / or having senior members of the organisation unaware if one exists suggests a disregard to quality in general.

Only 65.8% of those when asked about their companies' definition of quality were able to give a clear definition of how their company viewed quality. A further 23.7% of those that answered this question were unaware of any formal quality definition within their company. One in particular categorically stated that his company was not at all interested in quality but in fact "*values products that are developed cheaply and sold for more than they cost to develop. The company isn't interested in software quality at all. It's completely profit driven*". Another respondent who happened to be the managing director of the company stated "*No written definition, no. It's a small company*". The remaining 10.5% of respondents were unable to state what their companies definition was for quality but were able to speculate on what it was or what it should be.

For the company definitions of quality that were received, they did bear more than a passing resemblance to the personal quality definitions, with the majority of quality definitions focusing on meeting user requirements and the end user experience. For example, "*Producing a product that the customers want in a cost efficient way*" and "*Customer satisfaction, on time, error free, documented*". The chart in Figure 5.4. shows the breakdown of what the respondents viewed their company's definition of quality as.

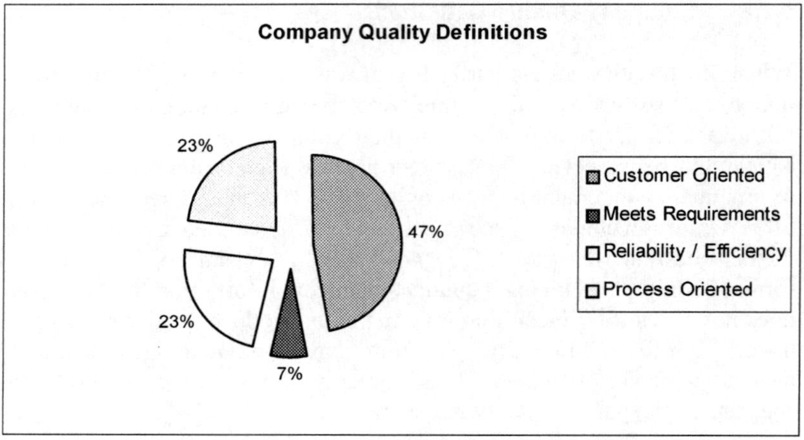

Figure 5.4. Breakdown of Company Quality Definitions

As can be seen from this pie chart, it bears a similarity to the pie chart presenting the respondent's personal views regarding quality. Customer oriented definitions form the primary answer given as was the case with the personal definitions. In the company definitions, the process-oriented definitions, reliability, deft and efficiency definitions were all equal at 23% each. However, only 7%, as compared with 15% of respondents stated that - in their view - meeting requirements was of highest importance when asked about their personal definition of quality.

As seen with the personal definitions regarding customer satisfaction, the company definitions fall into the same three areas of:

- Meeting the requirements or needs of the customer
- How the product performs for the customer
- Ensuring the customer gets value for money

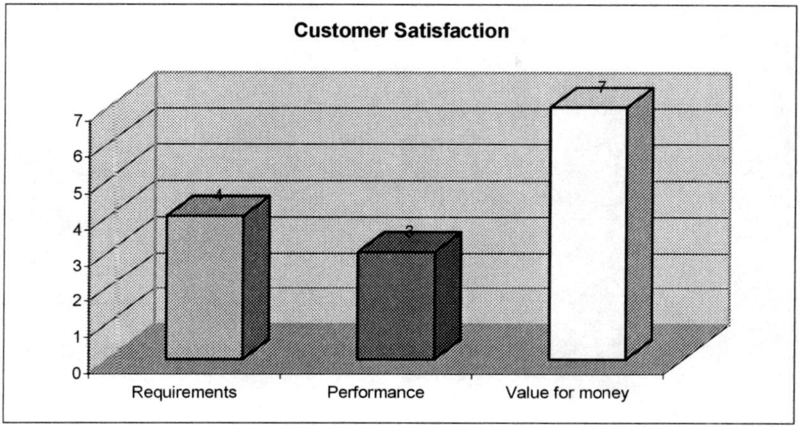

Figure 5.5. How to Satisfy Customers: Company

As can be seen in the chart above (Figure 5.5.), differences are again noted between the respondent's personal views and the views they have regarding their company. Meeting the requirement needs of a customer in order to satisfy them has dropped from 54% in the personal definitions to just 29% in the company view. Performance needs stays roughly the same at 26%, compared to 27% for the personal view. Customers getting "value for money" ranks highest for respondents as regards their company's attitude toward quality. This is over twice the amount reported from the respondent's personal views - at 50% as compared with just 19%.

5.2.5 Customer Type

As seen in the previous sections regarding individual and company perceptions of quality definitions; a high percentage of respondents offered answers centring on customer satisfaction. So who exactly are the customers that these organisations deal with? Interviewees were asked to categorise their customers i.e. whether they were internal or external. The pie chart below presents the information received.

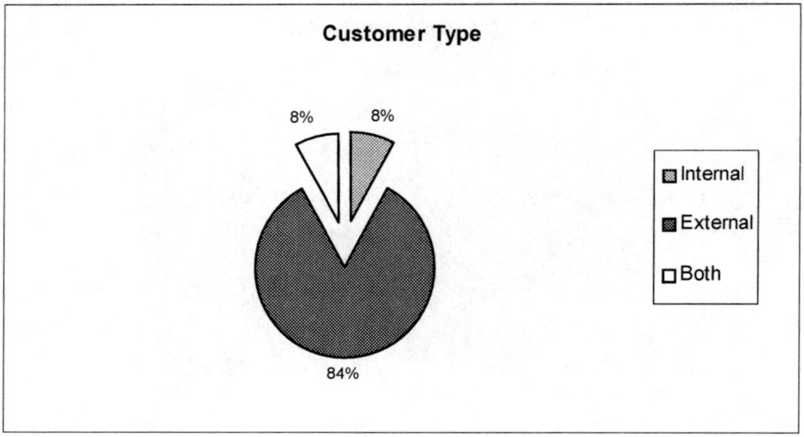

Figure 5.6. Customer Type of the Irish Software Industry

External customers dominate this pie chart (Figure 5.6.) with 84% of respondents exclusively catering for the needs of those outside their organisation. Nine percent catered exclusively for internal customers and 8% provided products or services for both internal and external customers at the same time.

Of the 91% of those who catered for external customers, customers fell into the following categories. In order of importance they are:

- IT Services
- Telecommunications industry
- Medical / pharmaceutical industry
- Government
- Automotive industry
- Construction / Engineering
- Financial services

The bar chart in Figure 5.7. presents the information received from interviewees regarding this. Some respondents worked in organisations that catered to multiple customers in various industries and this has been included in the bar chart. As can be seen from this chart the majority of external customers were in the IT services area. This area consists of customers *availing* of various IT services. The companies in this area were looking for various web-based services such as Internet sites and web-filtering products. Others were looking for software applications to use in their IT departments.

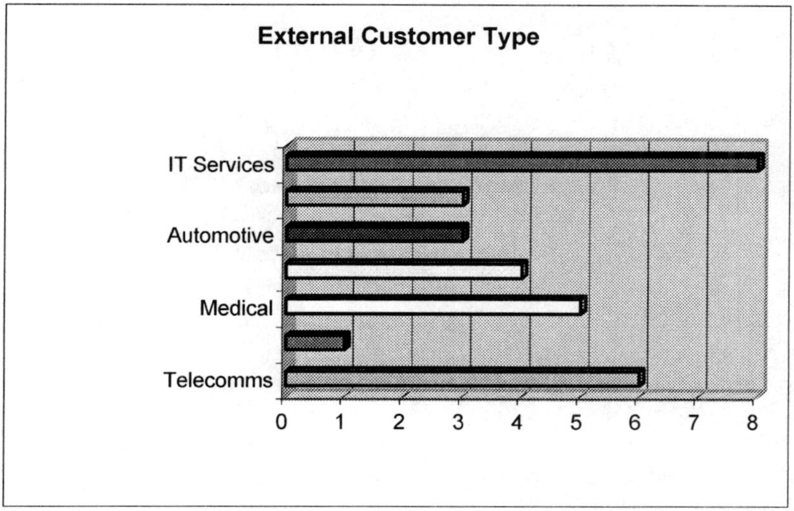

Figure 5.7. External Customer Type of the Irish Software Industry

5.2.6 Customer Attitudes towards Processes

Interviewees were then asked about their customer's views and attitudes towards software quality i.e. whether or not their customers knew or cared about what software processes were in place within the interviewee's organisations? Fifty one percent of interviewees responded by saying that their customers did not know or care about the software processes in operation. A further twenty-nine percent said that their customers did know about their software processes while a further 20% said that some of their customers did care while others did not care about the software processes in place. The chart in Figure 5.8. displays this in graphical format.

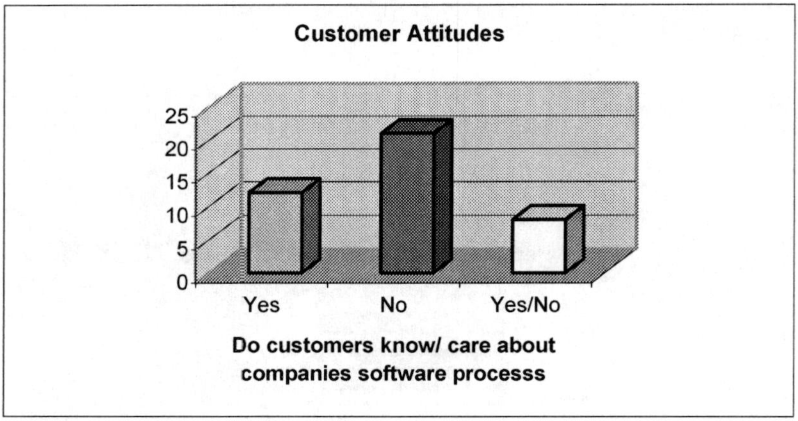

Figure 5.8. Customer Attitudes towards Software Process

For the 'no' category, some interviewees gave reasons as to why their customers either did not know or care about their software processes. These reasons included the following:

- *As long as they get a good product, on time and within budget, they are happy*
- *Our reputation for quality was enough to satisfy them*
- *Our customers only have a very basic – (if any) - IT knowledge*
- *The customers simply do not care about the processes.*

One particular interviewee stated that his company offered to show their customer how exactly they developed their products, but was told by the customer that he/she did not need to know.

For those customers that did care, a variety of reasons were given for their interests in the processes. Some customer organisations were involved in the medical industry, for example. This is a very heavily regulated industry particularly as regulated by the Food and Drug Administration (FDA), which lays down strict requirements on companies selling or using products in this industry. As a result, any company supplying products to a medical device company or to a company who supply such products would have to be regulated. In this situation it is absolutely necessary for customers to know what software processes are in place in the organisations that are supplying these types of products.

Other customers included those who were certified with an ISO standard or had achieved a particular CMM level. These customers insisted on knowing what software processes were in place. Some customers requested that particular organisations get certified or accredited in accordance with a particular software quality model prior to that customer doing business with them. Customers who were purchasing a particular product deemed critical to their operations would often insist on knowing about that organisation's software processes.

5.2.7 Customer Complaints

Customer complaints can be a day-to-day occurrence for some companies. But for all companies there exists a process or some method for dealing with customer complaints. Some companies have a more formal process than others for dealing with such complaints but the level of process appears to be dependent on the size of the organisation. It stands to reason that large organisations with multiple products and multiple customers would need a more formalised customer complaints process. For SME's, however, a less formal approach might be adopted. As stated previously, SME company employees may have a wide range of duties. In a large organisation it would be unusual for a CEO or top-level manager to be aware of the day-to-day complaints that customers might have. Due to the more compact nature of SME's, the top-level managers would sometimes be dealing personally with customers on these matters, however.

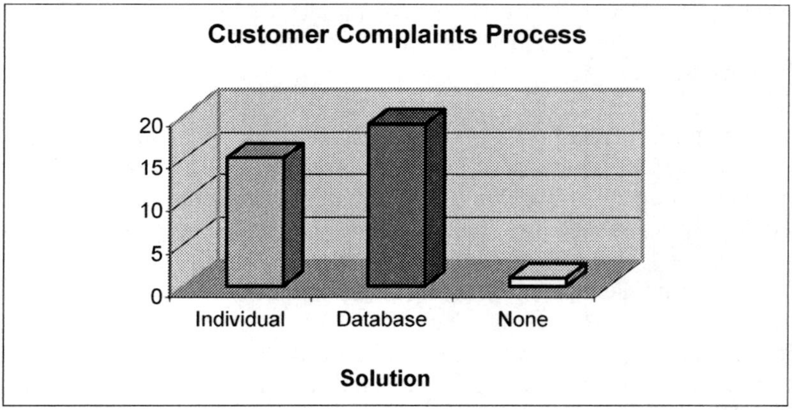

Figure 5.9. What is the Process to deal with Customer Complaints?

The bar chart in Figure 5.9. presents data received from interviewees regarding how they respond to customer complaints. Fifty four percent of respondents said that their organisation had either a database of customer issues or some formal defect-tracking system that logged customer complaints. Forty three percent of respondents dealt with customer complaints on an individual basis. This occurred for one of two reasons; either the issue was not a serious one and an individual developer was able to rectify it, or the company was an SME and it is in the nature of an SME to deal with customer problems on an individual basis. Only one interviewee who was a software developer stated that their company received no feedback on customer complaints either internally or externally. This interviewee went on to say that "*this is one of the most infuriating aspects of the job*". Receiving feedback is an important factor in any job, including that of a software developer. It lets them know whether they are doing things correctly, or if there's a mistake that it allows them to rectify it and learn from it.

Sixty nine percent of respondents said that their organisations offered technical support services to customers as well as dealing with issues on an individual basis or offering online defect tracking systems in order to help meet their customer needs. Another way of working with customers which some organisations utilised - was involving the customer in every stage of the development i.e. by getting the customer to "sign off" at the end of each development phase. Of course, this method may work quite well for those organisations developing a custom-built product for a customer that they already know; organisations developing off-the-shelf products for a wider customer base may not find this system as suitable for their needs.

Twenty three percent of respondents offered their opinions regarding which caused the majority of customer complaints. The main source of customer complaints appears to be in the requirements area. Incorrect requirements, changing requirements, or misunderstanding the requirements caused 75% of customer complaints. The remaining 25% stemmed from general customer misunderstandings as to how the product should or does work (see pie chart Figure 5.10). One may only presume that it is the responsibility of the supplier to ensure that their customer is fully informed as regards to the functionality of the product and that any misunderstandings are not the fault of the customer.

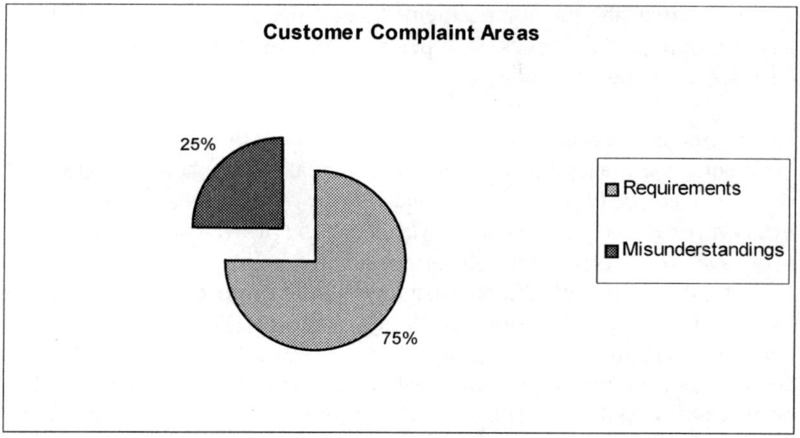

Figure 5.10. Customer Complaint Areas

5.2.8 Software Development Problems

Respondents were asked, "What are the main problems, which you encounter during software development?" Unsurprisingly, perhaps, requirements issues again topped the poll as the cause of most software development problems within the interviewee's organisations. Thirty-nine percent of respondents said that poor requirements capture or changing requirements caused them most problems. Respondents were also aware of the problems they had in getting their customers to specify their requirements and often found it hard to pin them down on specific requirements. Incorrect requirements or even poorly specified ones lead to problems further down the development track. Changing requirements at a later stage can often be one of the most expensive and time-consuming parts of developing a product.

Incorrect estimates were considered a major problem. Twenty-four percent of respondents view this as their most serious software development problem. Management were seen to be a big problem in this area, as deadlines were frequently seen to be too unrealistic and staff members were under constant pressure. "*They (management) would promise that it would be done in two weeks when we needed two months to do it*". This is a sentiment echoed by others who viewed inaccurate estimates as amongst their major software development problem "*If the timescales are unrealistic then problems can arise*". The estimation of these timelines and the management of customer expectations – (including overly-optimistic timelines) - appears to be causing concern within the Irish software industry today.

Management have their own views concerning the estimation process, however. One managing director, in particular, bemoaned his inability to receive a correctly-estimated project plan. "*Why can't I have a good estimate of development effort, why can't I have a good estimate of a project plan?*" This same managing director believes that the reason he cannot get a project plan is because this type of project planning is not yet in the nature of "normal"/everyday software development, "*Every developer will tell you, – "what we're doing is so innovative"*. It is as a consequence of this innovation that developers are unwilling to submit project plans. When developing a new product or using a new method – (though they may not always be in completely uncharted territory) - they developed are nevertheless frequently using new tools to navigate with. Therefore, they are unwilling to state how long it will take them to get to their end-destination, since they themselves are unsure of the answer.

Documentation was the third major problem highlighted by interviewees as a cause of their software development problems. Having an excessive amount of documentation can waste time that developers can instead spend on actual product development. Having too little documentation, however, can lead to variations in practice. In situations such as this, it is up to the individual to chose their own path regarding development or documentation procedures. This can lead to confusion across the board as each individual may have their own way of doing things, methods that may differ from one person to the next. Document control was also seen as important here. Having the latest, up-to-date document and maintaining it was difficult for some, while others found variations in the use of documentation to be a headache.

The chart in Figure 5.11. presents the issues discussed above – in and to - a lack of resources - as being amongst the major causes of software development problems in organisations. Other problems reported included:

- Internal Politics
- Use of new technology
- Testing procedures
- Lack of communication
- Lack of feedback from customers

- Maintenance
- Global software development issues

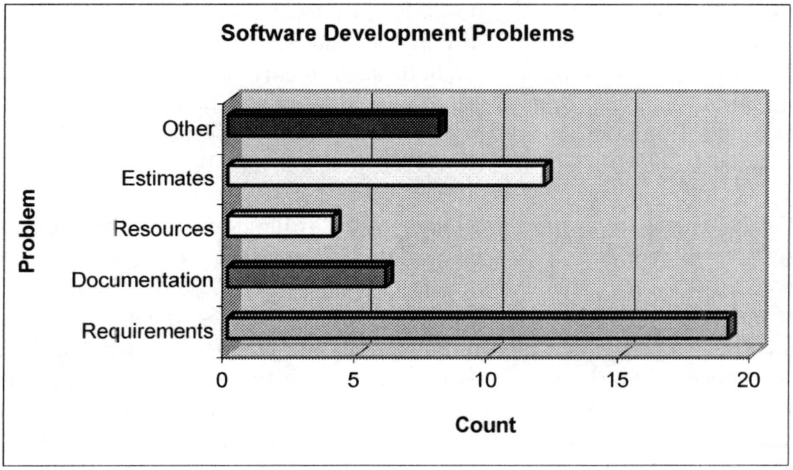

Fig 5.11. Software Development Problems

5.2.9 Solutions to Software Development Problems

Interviewees were then asked for their opinion regarding potential solutions to these problems. With regards to problems associated with requirements it was felt that more time needed to be dedicated to eliciting a more detailed specification from the customer. Having a streamlined requirements process was also considered a necessity. Even this was not seen as enough. Part of the problem with requirements is that they have a tendency to change. It is these changes that can cause major problems for organisations. Interviewees felt that requirements, once gathered, needed to be more rigid. There was also a need to ensure that customers did not drastically change their minds further down the line. To solve this, it was hoped to involve the customer from an early stage of the development especially with the requirements process and to have them as well as senior management sign off on any requirements documentation or change that might occur.

Interviewees had a wide range of potential solutions to the problem of incorrect estimation. Number one on their priority list was to communicate better with senior management. It is senior management that set the targets that developers have to meet. It is hoped by the interviewees that by involving senior management more, that they would learn to appreciate the difficulties associated with software development and as a result set more realistic deadlines. Having a standardised process was again identified as a potential solution to these problems. In the previous section on problems, a managing director gave his side of things when it came to estimates. The same managing director among others suggests a "project estimation tool" to help in giving better project estimations.

Documentation was the third major problem highlighted in the previous section. However there were variations in the exact problems associated with this. While some had problems with too much documentation, others reported the opposite in not enough documentation. Solutions offered for these problems again included having a formal process in place that deals with documentation issues. It was also suggested to educate employees with regard to the importance and correct use and maintenance of documents. Having a document control tool was seen as potential solution. For those that complained of having too much documentation having flexible, more informal procedures in place was seen as a way of solving this problem.

The issue of resources was a difficult one to find a solution to. Some interviewees suggest that having dedicated resources was the way to go here, but it was also necessary to inform the customer of these resources and make them aware of their capabilities. As with the previous three problems one of the solutions mentioned here was to have a formal process in place dealing with issues to do with resourcing. Having more resources is an obvious solution to having a lack of resources. However one interviewee in particular warned against rushing into this, "*There's a trade off point where a bit more investment will probably yield a better results, but you could definitely go too far and spend too much and not get back what you put into it*".

5.2.10 Software Process – Good

In the previous two sections, software development problems and their solutions as identified by interviewees were discussed. Interviewees were next asked to identify an example of a good software process in their organisation and if having a good software process in place positively affected the quality of the product being developed. Every respondent

(100%) said that having a good software process in place helps to improve product quality. The pie chart below shows the breakdown of good software processes as identified by interviewees.

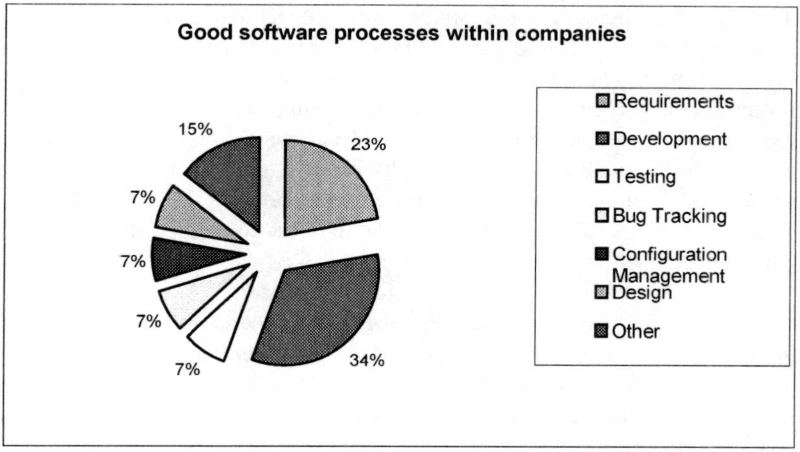

Figure 5.12. Examples of Good Software Process

As can be seen from this chart (see Figure 5.12.), 34% of respondents listed their company's development process as an example of a good software process within their organisation. Respondents were asked why this process was considered a good one? Varying answers were given to this question. Some respondents claimed the development process was good because *"when followed it produces good results". Others stated that the development process was "engrained within the organisation, offering key deliverables, was well documented and covered risk management."*

One respondent claimed that the development process was good because of the previous experience of the software engineers in this area. However, this author feels that a process is not necessarily a good one just because the people following it are experienced. One of the ideas behind having a structured process in place is that someone new to the organisation should be able to come in and easily get up to speed. Though experience with processes would help, it should not be a necessity. Yes, people need to be trained and educated with regard to structured processes and their benefits. However, just because a software engineer is experienced; in relation to software development, this does not mean that he or she is experienced with software processes. By having an experienced team in place, it does not follow that the processes will be efficient, even if the product is itself an excellent product.

Twenty-three percent of respondents highlighted their requirements process as an example of a good software process within their organisation. The most common explanation for why this particular requirements process was considered a good one was put down to experience, i.e. the experience of the individuals following the process in addition to the experience generated by efficacy of the process itself. One respondent singled out the requirements process in his particular organisation as a relatively efficient one and yet confirmed that it was far from perfect.

This respondent stated: "*The one drawback is that customers are not involved very much in the requirements gathering until after the first requirements document has been approved by us*". The respondent went on to say that the time and effort already spent on these processes could come to nothing if the customer (at this point) changed their mind.

It was interesting that although the requirements process was held up as a good software process in 23% of organisations, it was nevertheless seen to cause the majority of software development problems for organisations. When examined further it was found that 33% of those who said that requirements-gathering was one of their better processes, also listed the requirements phase as their top software development problem! There seems to be a contradiction here. Thirty-three per cent said that incorrect estimates were at the root of their software development problems. These respondents also pointed out the fact that estimates became a problem "especially if requirements change". Seventeen percent listed poor communication as their main software development problem, while the remaining 17% had not given sufficient information regarding their software development problems. This means that 66% of those who said that their requirements process was a good one had also listed requirements - or a problem relating to or caused by requirements changes - as their primary software development problem. The pie chart (Figure 5.13.) presents this information in graphical format.

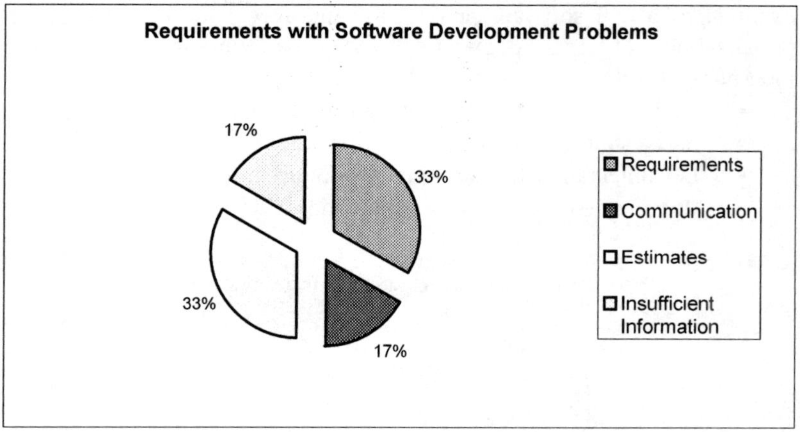

Figure 5.13. Good Requirements with Software Development Problems

5.2.11 Software Process – Bad

Having given examples and reasons behind what makes a particular software process a good one, interviewees were asked to do the same for a bad software process within their organisation. Ninety one percent of respondents said that having a bad software process in place helps to decrease product quality. However 9% of respondents disagreed with this assessment - a small cohort of people who provided the following reasons for their views. One respondent claimed that a manual testing process was followed in his organisation, as opposed to an automated and quicker testing process. While there was nothing wrong with this manual process it was deemed "*just too expensive for us to do*". Another respondent who disagreed with the proposition that a bad process reduces product quality said, "*you can have extremely good people that can develop a good product, but it's luck*". The respondent went on to say that "*what a good process gives you is consistency*". It is this consistency that can almost guarantee a minimum level of quality each time, without relying on luck.

The pie chart in Figure 5.14. presents what the respondents identified as bad software processes within their organisations. Perhaps unsurprisingly, given the problems reported with requirements and the focus on requirements in the interviewee and company quality definitions, requirements issues were identified as the worst offender. Thirty seven percent of respondents said that the requirements process was their example of a bad software process as employed within their particular organisation. The reasons given as to why the requirements phase often incorporated bad software processes:

- Multiple people involved in sign-off causes complexity
- Skills shortage in eliciting requirements
- Documentation for requirements not up to scratch
- Requirements needs constant revision

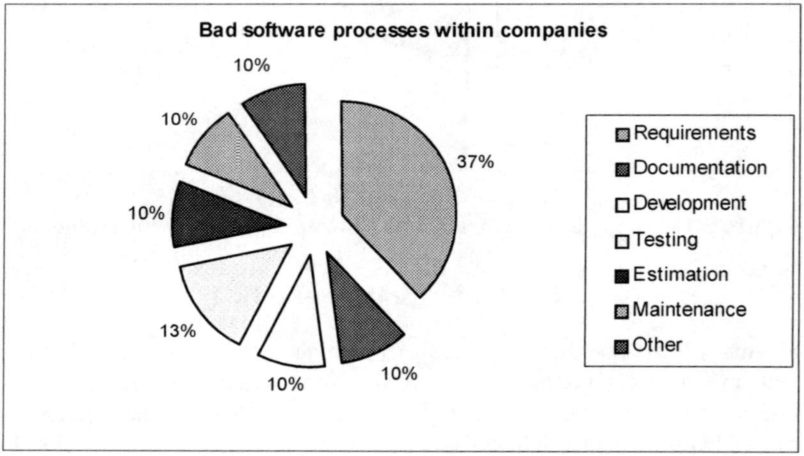

Figure 5.14. Examples of Poor Software Processes in Organisations

The next highest offender on the list, with 13% of respondents identifying it as a bad software process - was the testing process. Some respondents felt that there was never enough time spent on testing. Others cited having no dedicated testers due to financial constraints as a problem. This resulted in a situation where the people who had designed the product were also testing it - which is *"a bad idea"*. Another respondent wanted an automated test process to be put in place, as this would *"reduce the time and cost of exercising it prior to each release"*.

Documentation, development, estimation and maintenance were all equal offenders - with 10% of respondents each – all of whom cited these processes as examples of a bad software process within their respective organisations. Other software process identified as bad ones included:

- Version control
- Reviews

In the previous section it was noted that although 23% of respondents listed requirements as an example of a good software process, 66% of those respondents said that requirements was their main software development problem. This time, the results were slightly different, however. In total, 37% of respondents highlighted their requirements process as an example of a bad software process within their organisation. The research then compared these poor software processes against what the respondents stated to be their primary software development problems. The results are presented in the pie chart (see Figure 5.15.).

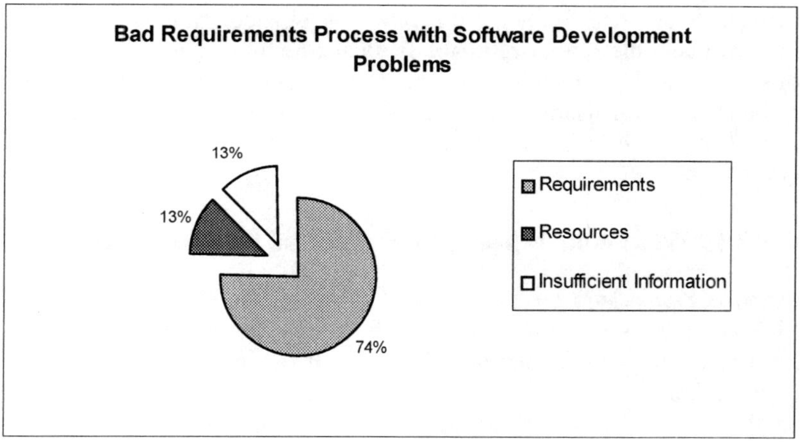

Figure 5.15. Bad Requirements with Software Development Problems

As can be seen from this pie chart, 74% of those that listed requirements as an example of a bad software process also identified requirements as their main software development problem. Thirteen percent of respondents listed resources as their main software development problem. However, when examined further it was revealed that that this lack of resources was causing problems in terms of eliciting requirements. In summary then, 87% of those giving requirements as an example of their bad software process, also directly or indirectly listed requirements as their main software development problem. The remaining 13% had insufficient information to categorise the exact nature of their software development problems. There is a clear consistency of response here with a 100% correlation between companies with a bad requirements process - and who also identify requirements as their main software development problem.

5.2.12 Why do some Irish software organisations not implement any software quality model?

Irish interview respondents whose companies were not using any software quality model gave a variety of reasons to justify this. Some respondents argued that they were too small a company and that any one of these models would be too costly and involve too many overheads for them to implement. Other organisations – (while not using any formal model) - were using individuals experiences in relation to various processes. Such a system is naturally overly-reliant on particular individuals workers, however. It provides no back-up if this person were to fall ill or leave the company. Anyone following on from – or replacing this person, would have to know the processes this individual was following - assuming that this individual was following these processes to the letter. Other respondent's organisations never saw the need to have a quality model in place because "*customers don't ask about it, they don't seem to be aware of it*".

5.2.13 What models are used in the Irish software industry?

Data from interviews

The pie chart (see Figure 5.16) shows the data received from the Irish interviews regarding the various different software quality models used by organisations. ISO standards are by far the most commonly used software quality models accounting for 45% of the total used. Tick IT was next popular with 17% of respondents using this model in their organisation. The Capability Maturity Model accounted for only 13% of the total models used. Other models used included:

- PACE
- CMMI
- GAMP
- FURPS+
- Corbet

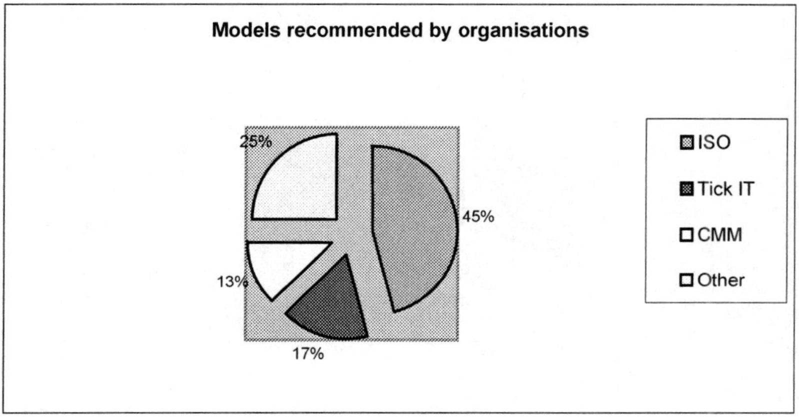

Figure 5.16. Which model is recommended for use by your organisation?

Data from questionnaires

Separate research conducted in the form of an online questionnaire provides a different but useful perspective regarding adoption rates of quality models within the Irish Software Industry (see Appendix K). A list of quality models was presented and respondents to the survey were asked whether they had experience with using any of them. Respondents were asked to categorise their experience based on five choices:

- No experience
- Am familiar with concepts
- Have worked with it
- Have evaluated it
- Have implemented it

The pie chart in Figure 5.17 shows the information received regarding the ISO 9000:1994 standard. Thirty five percent of respondents had implemented this standard, while a further 28% had either worked with the standard or evaluated it. Seventeen percent had no experience what-so-ever with the standard and 20% were only familiar with the concepts of the standard. The ISO 9000:1994 standard has been replaced by the ISO 9000:2000 standard. As a result, it may be assumed that those new to the software industry would possible have little or no experience with the standard, but may have experience with its replacement.

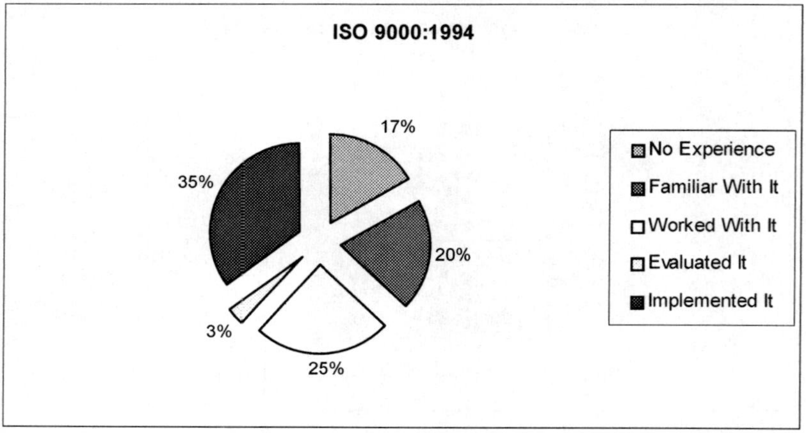

Figure 5.17. Experience with ISO 9000:1994

The pie chart below (see Figure 5.18) represents the newer version of this ISO standard i.e. ISO 9000:2000. Twenty percent of respondents have experience implementing ISO 9000:2000. Twenty percent have either worked with the standard or evaluated it. Twenty seven percent have no experience with the standard while 30% are familiar with its basic concepts.

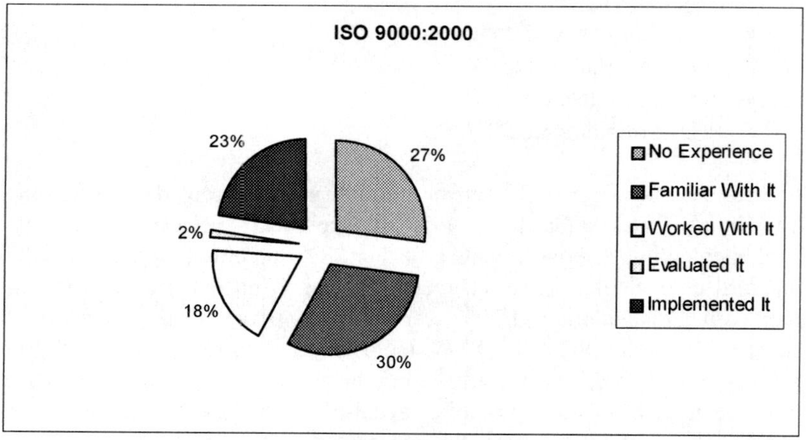

Figure 5.18. Experience with ISO 9000:2000

Based on the information gathered from the interviews, the majority of respondents (45%) had some experience with the ISO series of standards. This popularity was again evident in the results of the online questionnaire. No other quality model or standard – (according to the online questionnaire) - had a higher implementation percentage, though both standard types did fall short of the level of implementation evident amongst the interviewees.

Results from the interviewees highlighted Tick IT as the second most widely-used quality model or standard. This same level of popularity was attributed to Tick IT after analysing the information received from the online questionnaire. This information is presented in the pie chart in Figure 5.19. Fifteen percent of respondents to the online questionnaire had experience implementing Tick IT, compared with 17% - as based on the interviewee's organisations. Only 9% had either worked with or evaluated the model. Fifteen percent of respondents were familiar with the concepts of the model while the majority of the respondents (61%) had no experience with it.

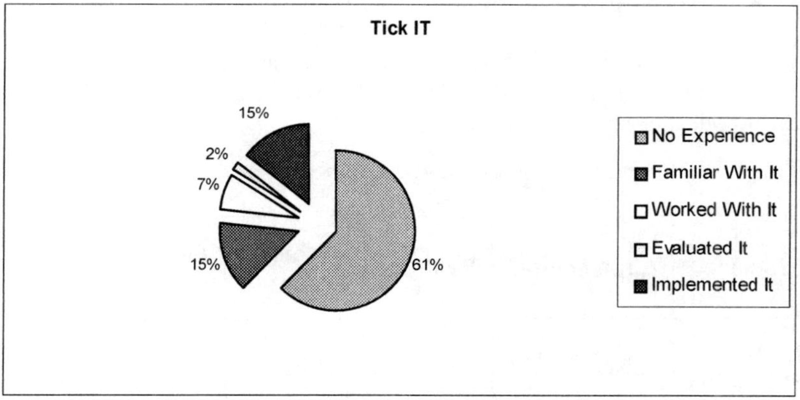

Fig 5.19. Experience with Tick IT

The CMM was found to be the third most implemented model among the questionnaire respondents, although not by much. The pie chart in Figure 5.20 presents the information received regarding CMM. As can be seen, only 6% of respondents have implemented this model. Twenty nine percent were found to have worked with or evaluated this model at some stage or other. Thirty percent were familiar with the concepts of the model while 35% had no experience with it at all.

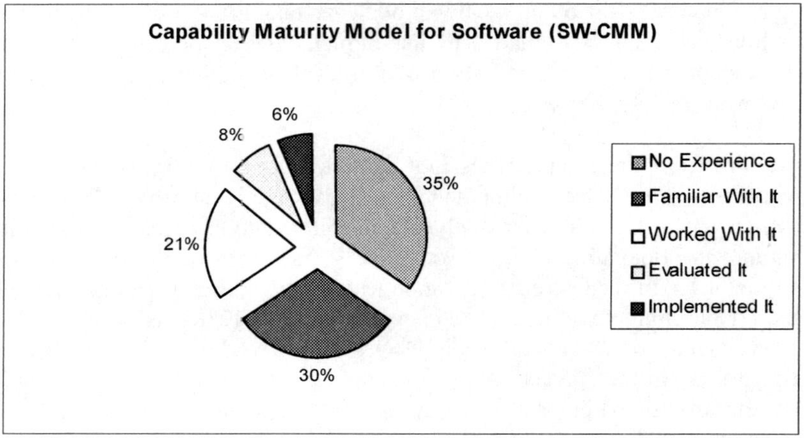

Figure 5.20. Experience with Capability Maturity Model

The following table (table 5.3) summarises the data received from selected quality models. For a complete list of the frequency tables as relating to each model surveyed, see Appendix L:

Table 5.3. Summary of quality model experience

Model	**Implemented**	**Evaluated**	**Worked with**	**Familiar with**	**No experience**
ISO 9000:1994	35%	3%	25%	20%	17%
ISO 9000:2000	23%	2%	18%	30%	27%
Tick IT	15%	2%	7%	15%	61%
SW-CMM	6%	8%	21%	30%	35%

CMMI	5%	5%	12%	29%	49%
Six Sigma	6%	5%	6%	39%	44%
SPICE	0%	0%	2%	10%	88%

5.2.14 Summary

Based on the data gathered from both the interviews and the online questionnaire, it can be seen that the ISO series of standards appears to be the most popular quality framework in use within the Irish software industry. Despite the popularity of the ISO standards, one worrying fact remains. Quality models are not in widespread use in Ireland. In fact, based on the table of data (above) - it is evident that a high percentage of software professionals have little or no experience whatsoever with many of these different software quality models.

5.3 Conclusion

Interviews were conducted within the Irish software community with members of various software engineering companies - ranging from those at CEO level to the software engineers themselves. It was found that the majority of these workers were well-educated, possessing (at least) an undergraduate third-level qualification – and with many pursuing further postgraduate studies. The Irish software community is clearly a skilled workforce with a high concentration of well-educated people. This augurs well for the Irish software industry of the future and could potentially be utilised as a more effective marketing tool.

The quality definitions of those interviewed were then examined. The majority of personal quality definitions centred on the idea of pleasing or satisfying the needs of a customer. When further examined, satisfying the needs of a customer usually meant meeting the requirements of the customer or user i.e. giving them a high-performing product and/or giving them value for money. When compared against what interviewees gave as their company's definition of quality the result was quite similar, with the majority of companies having a quality definition centring on the customer. One worrying fact that emerged from this was the ignorance of some of the interviewees as to their own company's quality definition. It raises the question as to how focused these companies are on quality, given that many of their own employees do not know what quality means to them.

Research then focused on the customers of the Irish software industry. Customers came from a variety of different industries including; telecommunications, governmental agencies, and the automotive and medical industries. One interesting and worrying fact that emerged here was the widespread disregard which customers often had towards the processes that were in place within these individual software organisations. The majority of customers did not know and did not want to know what software process their vendor had. Customer complaints records were examined and were found to be mainly requirements based. Issues with poor or changing requirements caused the majority of problems for customers as well as misunderstandings over general product use.

The primary cause of software development problems in the Irish software industry were a particular focus at this stage of the research. Requirements again appeared on the radar with the majority of organisations reporting requirements-related issues as the cause of their main software development problems. Issues with poor project estimation in addition to incorrect or inadequate use of documentation were also to blame for organisations' software development problems. Solutions to these problems were discussed including: standardised processes, improved communications and the improved education/training of company employees.

The interviewees each gave examples of good and bad software processes, as they had experienced them. Each respondent confirmed that having a good software process positively affects product quality and the development and requirements processes were identified as good examples of software process within the majority of organisations. The majority of respondents - as relating to their own companies – gave examples of both the requirements and the testing processes.

CHAPTER SIX

FOCUS ON QUALITY: INDIA AND IRELAND

6.1 Introduction

A high focus on quality and quality processes is one of the advantages that the Indian software industry uses in its attempt to garner more business. One of the ways Indian companies demonstrate their high focus on quality is through maturity ratings and certification as incorporated within a variety of software quality models. For software organisations in Indian, the question is not - "will we implement a software quality model?" – butrahter "which model do we implement and how do we implement it?"

Certification or maturity ratings do not guarantee success, of course. They do however demonstrate to potential clients that the certified organisation has demonstrated mature and capable processes. By doing this, Indian software organisations offer their potential clients some security in the knowledge that structured processes are in place and need to be followed for the production of whatever product or service that the vendor supplies. Indian software organisations have recognised the need to be able to demonstrate mature processes and can, in addition boast a low-cost and highly-skilled workforce, who are adept at offering a high quality process.

6.2 Software Quality Models

6.2.1 Are Software Quality Models used?

Within software organisations in India the belief is that if you want to compete and stay in business, you must implement a quality model. Indian software professionals believe that there is no choice in this matter. Either have a quality model and compete for those lucrative business process-outsourcing (BPO) contracts or go out of business. The only choice for Indian software organisations may lie in which model to implement or how much of the model to implement.
From the research conducted in Ireland, the situation was found to be different. Irish interviewees were asked whether or not their company

used a recognised software quality model. The pie chart (see Figure 6.1) below presents this information. As can be seen from this, 52% of respondents stated that their companies used a recognised quality model. Eleven percent of respondents said that while they did not use a recognised quality model, they followed their own internal processes. However 37% of respondents to this question said that they did not follow a software quality model or have their own internal processes.

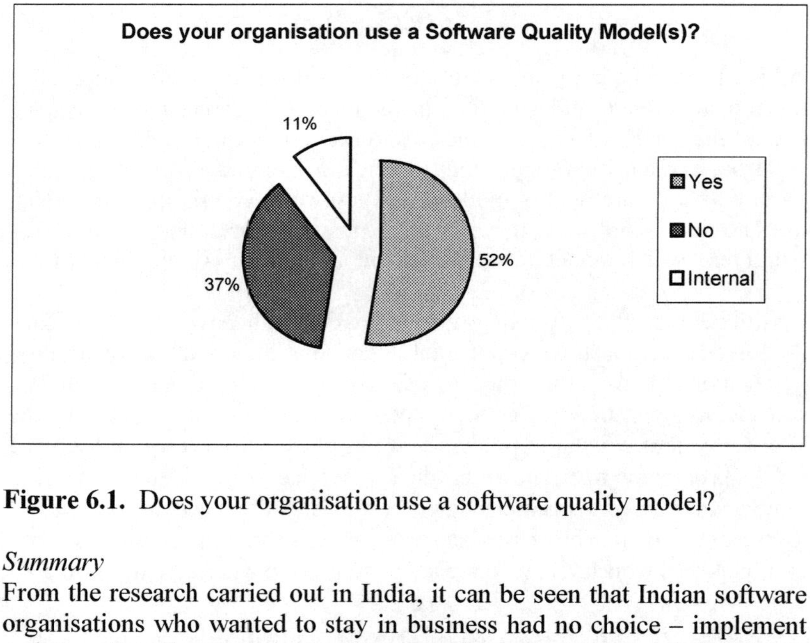

Figure 6.1. Does your organisation use a software quality model?

Summary
From the research carried out in India, it can be seen that Indian software organisations who wanted to stay in business had no choice – implement an internationally-recognised software quality model or go out of business. However the situation in Ireland appears to be vastly different. Only 52% have implemented a recognised model, and 37% have no such framework, formal or otherwise in place.

6.2.2 Why are particular Software Quality Models used?

In India, the choice of which model to implement was dictated either by market forces, customer requirements or both. CMM is a globally-recognised and widely-used quality model, particularly in the United States of America (USA). Since the USA is the originating source for the majority of outsourcing to India, it makes sense for Indian software organisations to implement the CMM. Similarly, a direct customer requirement was a major influencing factor for Indian software organisations as regards which quality model to implement.

For those Irish software organisations that did follow a recognised software quality model, there were three primary reasons behind the models used. As can be seen from the pie chart – (see Figure 6.2), 47% of those interviewees whose organisations were using a software quality model viewed market forces as their reason for the use of a particular model

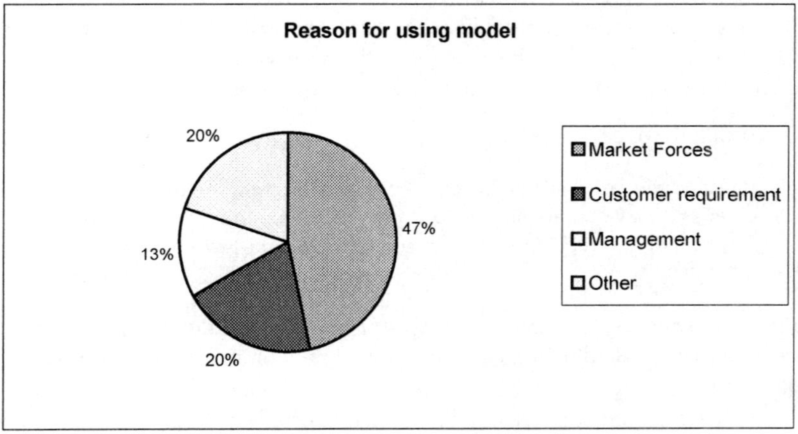

Figure 6.2. What was the reason behind using a particular quality model?

However if those organisations already in the industry have a particular certification, new entrants stood a better chance of competing if they could at least match up to their competitors' demonstrated quality processes (Keane and Richardson, 2004).

Organisations realise that some models are more applicable to certain cultures and environments than others. One organisation which is currently operating in the European market but trying to gain entry to the market in the USA has ISO 9000 accreditation and is attempting to get certified at level 3 in CMM. Their view is that "*the CMM is more recognised in the States than in Europe... so we'll have the European ISO and an American CMM*". While this view may not be accurate in the literal sense, the ISO series of standards are viewed as more of a European standard while the CMM is viewed as being more practical for the markets operating in the USA. For this reason those companies wishing to break into the American markets would be advised to pursue a CMM certification to help them achieve their business goals.

A direct request or requirement from a customer cannot be taken lightly. This is particularly the case if the customer is considered an important one, or if the organisation receiving the request is a small-medium enterprise relying on a core group of customers for its business. Twenty percent of respondents said that the reason for their organisation using a software quality model was due to their customer. Some customers will only do business with those companies that can demonstrate mature processes. One way of doing this is by being certified in accordance with a particular standards body or by having achieved a particular maturity level.

According to one respondent:

> "Our customers don't have clear visibility at times into our process because it may be only once a year they get an opportunity to visit us. So they regard ISO registration as being a key indicator that our quality is up to scratch."

Pressure from senior management was also an important factor for 20% of interviewees. Senior management in some companies recognised the danger of having non-existent processes and in having their employees "*doing things their own way*". To solve this problem they pushed the idea of a quality model as a potential solution. However, this did not always work out and in one case it was found "*difficult to handover any tasks as most of the information was in the head of the person doing it*". The literature advises organisations - depending on their particular circumstances - to start an improvement programme based on a process or set of processes, and then to roll this out to the rest of the organisation. This method can demonstrate the benefits of such a programme to both staff and management and keep them focused on continued improvement (Wiegers, 1999).
The remaining 20% of respondents offered different reasons as to why their organisation chose to use a particular model. These reasons included:

- Size of the project or organisation
- Business Goals
- Customer Satisfaction

Summary

Market forces and customer requirements were the two main influencing factors for Irish software organisations choosing to implement a quality model, a situation similar to that found in Indian software organisations. In India, these were the only two reasons behind implementing a software quality model. However, in the Irish software industry, other factors also played a part:

- Management-driven implementation
- Size of the project or organisation
- Business Goals
- Customer Satisfaction

The situation in Indian appears to be more definite. Implement a quality model or go out of business - and the quality model chosen is usually dictated by market forces and/or direct customer requirements.

6.2.3 Why were some models not pursued if evaluated?

Indian software professionals gave two reasons as to why certain models were not pursued, even if they had been evaluated. If there was no tangible benefit that a particular quality model could bring to an organisation or, if the model's practices were to be implemented solely to satisfy the model and not the business needs of the organisation, then the model would not be implemented.

The majority of Irish respondents (49%) said that the model evaluated was either too costly or too difficult to implement. Thirty-three percent said that the model was too prescriptive (e.g. detailed, inflexible). Thirteen percent said that the quality model evaluated was not suitable for software development within their particular organisation and 5% said that the model was not prescriptive enough (e.g. too broad, not enough substance) (see Figure 6.3).

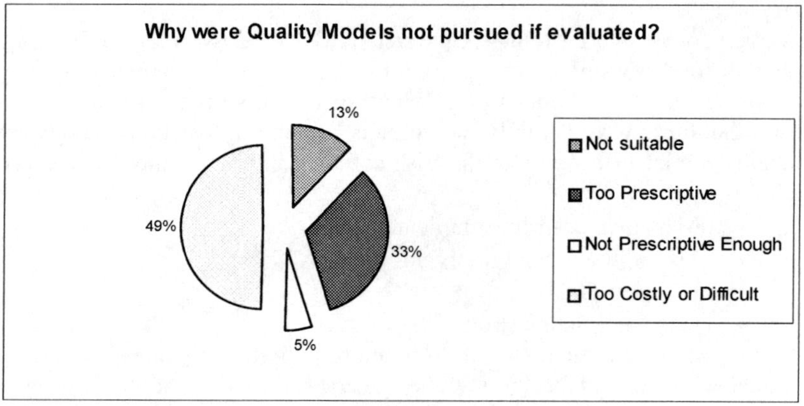

Figure 6.3. Why were some models not pursued if evaluated?

Summary
Again, the situation in India is found to be straightforward. If the quality model cannot provide enough tangible benefits, or does not suit the business needs of the organisation, an organisation will not implement the model. In Ireland, the main reason for not implementing a model is cost or difficulty. It can be costly for organisations to implement a quality model, and depending on the model, it can be expensive to get certified or audited for specific levels. This is equally as expensive for Indian organisations, yet they are embracing the idea of quality models more readily than their Irish counterparts.

6.3 Focus on quality

6.3.1 Indian Situation

Indian software organisations have recognised the need to demonstrate mature and transparent processes. Software quality models or frameworks allow for international accreditation or certification from independent bodies. They do not guarantee success or quality but they do offer potential vendors the knowledge of structured processes. Indian software organisations have enthusiastically embraced the concept of quality models because they see the competitive advantage that they offer.

Improvement does not stop there. Any software process improvement initiative should be implemented on a continuous basis. Indian software organisations recognise this and continually investigate new or improved quality models or frameworks that can be implementated in their organisations. Indian software organisations do not stop after implementing a single quality model, however. They look around and seek the best that is on offer, and they implement or tailor 'the best' to suit the needs of their particular organisation - thereby continually refining their focus on quality.

6.3.2 Irish situation

6.3.2.1 Software organisations

Respondents were asked a number of questions that are related to how focused both they and their customers are on quality. The first of these questions was - "Is there a dedicated quality manager in your organisation?" This question had a 100% response rate. Fifty four percent had a dedicated quality manager in their organisation, leaving a high number of companies (46%) without a dedicated quality manager. It could be argued that perhaps some of those who said no were employed in small firms. In these situations, although there may not be an individual dedicated to quality, there is an individual responsible for quality in addition to various other duties. However this was not always the case.

Respondents were asked how many employees were in their organisation. Only 26% of respondents worked in organisations with less than 50 employees. The majority of respondents (38%) worked in organisations with 50-250 employees. Eighteen percent worked in organisations employing 250-500. The remaining 18% were employed in organisations with more than 500 employees. With only 26% employed in organisations with less than 50 employees, this leaves a minimum of 20% of organisations that are not considered small and yet are without a dedicated quality manager.

The second question relating to organisations' focus on quality was - "Do you have a quality road map in place?" Sixty-four percent said no. Coupled with the disappointing figures regarding dedicated quality managers, this suggests an attitude of disregard among certain sections of the software community in Ireland towards the issue of quality process.

6.3.2.2 Customers

It appears that Irish software organisations are not the only ones that show a disregard or lack of knowledge towards software processes. Customers also show a lack of awareness regarding the benefits to their suppliers - of employing quality models or structured processes. Respondents were asked "how often are you requested about being certified on a particular quality model during the sales process?" They were then given 5 choices to choose from:

- 0-20%
- 20%-40%
- 40%-60%
- 60%-80%
- 80%-100%

The bar chart below (see Figure 6.9) presents the information received from this question, which received a 94% response rate. The majority of respondents, i.e. 45 in total - said that they were only asked about certification between 0-20% of times, when making a sale. Twelve respondents said they were asked between 20%-40% of the time, on average. Eight respondents were asked between 40%-60% of the time, while 3 respondents said they were asked between 60%-80% of the time. Only 4 respondents had enquires from customers regarding their quality model certification – i.e. between 80%-100% of the time and during the sales process.

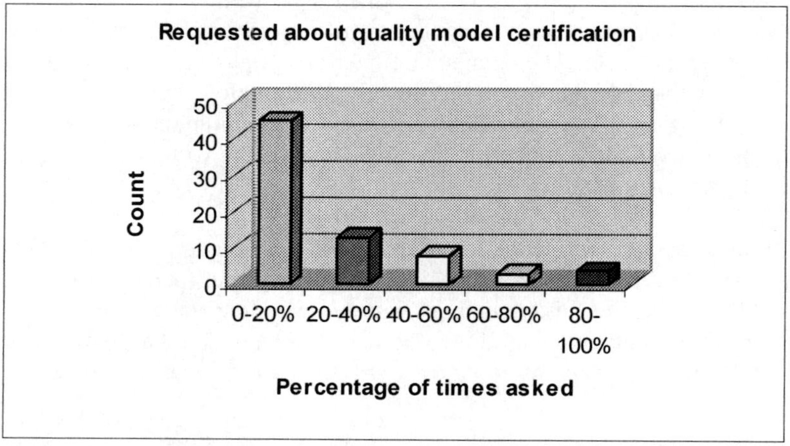

Figure 6.4. Requests about quality model certification

Seventy-one percent of respondents to the online questionnaire were employed in an indigenous organisation with the remaining 29% in a subsidiary of a multinational organisation. A comparison was done between those being requested about certification as compared with the type of organisation they worked in. As can be seen from the chart below, (see Figure 6.10) the large majority of indigenous organisations (35% or 70%) are only asked between 0-20% of times during the sales process - whether or not they are certified with any quality model. Only 15 (30%) out of the 50 indigenous organisations are being asked on a more regular basis. With the multinationals there some differences. A smaller majority of 48% is noted here for those who are requested for certification between 0%-20% of the time. This leaves 52% of multinationals who are asked about certification on a more regular basis.

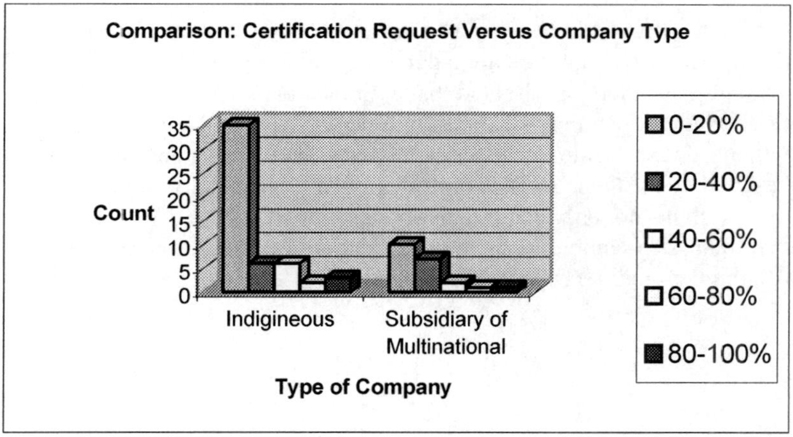

Figure 6.5. Certification request Vs Type of company

Without further research, the reasons for the differences found here can only be speculated upon. However, one possibility is that multinational organisations may be dealing with customers not only in Ireland but also as relating to larger markets in Europe, the United States and Asia. In this scenario they would be advised to have structured repeatable processes in place, so as to meet the demands of different worldwide markets on a consistent basis. It may also be the case that the majority of indigenous software organisations, which are small to medium enterprises, deal almost exclusively with the Irish market. In this situation they may believe that they do not need nor want to have either a quality model or standardised processes in place. However, this is only speculation and further research would be necessary to explore these issues more thoroughly.

6.3.2.3 Summary

One of the selling points of the Indian software industry is its high focus on quality. This is demonstrated through the use and implementation of quality models and their capability to adapt to particular environments. Members of the Indian software community have recognised the ability of quality models and frameworks to demonstrate structured processes to potential vendors. This represents a focus on quality on their part, one which is also a very useful marketing tool.

The Irish software industry may have established itself before the Indian software industry, but they are lagging behind in the quality stakes. While some organisations in Ireland have implemented a recognised quality model there still remains a large number of Irish software organisations without one. While these organisations may cite numerous business reasons behind their decision not to implement a quality model, the fact remains that - not only can Indian organisations claim to offer a lower cost than their Irish competitors - they can, through certification, also claim to offer higher quality products and services.

CHAPTER SEVEN

CONCLUSIONS AND RECOMMENDATIONS

7.1 Introduction

The conclusion to this volume is divided into four sections. The first section provides a brief summary of the volume, chapter by chapter. Secondly, the reflections of the author regarding the results obtained from the attitudes towards quality of the Irish and Indian software industries are presented. The third section discusses the various recommendations made, recommendations which are based on the research undertaken to date. This section is focuses on software organisations as a whole and small-to-medium-sized software firms, in particular. Finally, a brief conclusion to the volume is provided.

7.2 Summary of volume

One of the aims of this research project was to examine the attitudes and experiences of the software industry in Ireland towards quality and software processes. Research was also conducted within various Indian software organisations as relating to their selection and use of software quality models. Similar research was also carried out in an Irish context and the results were then compared. The apparent focus on quality in the official "rhetoric" of each country's software industry was also discussed.

A literature review was undertaken to give the author a wider knowledge base of the quality area in general, the various approaches to quality, quality management systems, software process improvement and software quality models. Research phases were carried out in India and in the Republic of Ireland. Research methodologies specific to each phase were discussed as well as tools used to aid in the analysis of data collected. The focus of this research project changed over time; how this change occurred and what it meant to the research project is also presented.

Chapter four presents the results from the research carried out in India, with the aid of an Indian software-consulting firm. An introduction to the

Indian software industry is also provided. This phase of the research focused on software quality models – i.e. their selection and use within the Indian software industry. Specifically, what prompts an organisation to seek change and implement a quality model is examined. Also investigated are the reasons why some models are considered for selection but not implemented and what an organisation needs to consider when implementing a software quality model.

Chapter five focuses on the Irish research results. An introduction to the Irish software industry is given as well as a background to the members of the Irish software community. Individual and company quality definitions from the interviewees are examined. The customers of the Irish software industry, their attitudes towards the software process and their areas of main complaint are discussed. Software development problems experienced by the industry are investigated as well as examples and opinions regarding what makes a good/ bad software process.

Chapter six presents the results of a comparison made between selected data collected from the Irish software industry and the Indian software industry. This comparison centres on both industry's selection and use of software quality models and their respective attitudes towards quality.

7.3 Attitudes Towards Quality

The Irish Software Industry is very much a product-based industry aimed towards export. According to Ryan (2005) The Irish Software Ecosystem focuses high on the value-chain in particular as relating to product design and marketing. He goes on to say that the industry is export-oriented and has a good reputation. On the other hand, "India's offshore sector, the world's largest and fastest growing is dominated by IT services, which play a major role in the country's overall economic growth" (Farrell, Kaka et al., 2005). So if these two nation's software industries focus on different aspects of software, should the service-based Indian software industry be a cause for concern for the product-based Irish software industry?

It is not for the researcher to answer this question; however, this study has shown that attitudes to software quality differ and this researcher considers that it should be a cause for concern for the Irish software industry. The Indian software industry has built its reputation based on its provision of services. The Irish software industry has built its own reputation based around its ability to design and produce products. Both industries rely on reputation as a selling point and quality, be it service or product based, forms the basis for these reputations.

This researcher believes that quality can be an area where the Irish software industry may be able to compete with their Indian counterparts for those lucrative FDI deals. Research was undertaken and interviews were conducted with members of the Irish software community. From the quality perspective, initial findings in the Irish software industry are worrying. They suggest an attitude of disregard within some sections of the software community towards software quality. Quality in Ireland was traditionally only applied to manufacturing industry as outside of farming given that was the latter was the basis for most industries within the country. The software industry in Ireland has grown considerably in the last 20 years, from moving an almost non-entity to its current prosperous state in the era of the Celtic Tiger. This growth is largely due to the investment in the Irish software industry by large multi – national corporations. However, in spite of this growth, growth which has made Ireland one of the most recognised exporters of software in the world, it still appears that quality processes and procedures have been largely ignored.

There is a definite feeling within some software organisations that senior management do not know and do not want to know about the software process in place within their organisation. The same is true for customer organisations whose primary business may not be in the software industry, but who nevertheless use software products. Top-level management in some of these Irish organisations do not wish to know how their product was built or what processes are in place within the organisation that built it. As long as the product gets to them on time, at the agreed price, and is reliable, they do not care about the capability of the process' involved, because they often do no know what that means.

Top-level managers seem ignorant towards the benefits of software process improvement techniques. Were they to see the importance of process improvement initiatives and what they can bring to their organisation, they might begin to re-evaluate their importance. One interviewee worked in a multinational company with bases in Ireland and India among other countries. The company's Irish base was not CMM-certified nor were they pursuing it. The interviewee pointed out that "*the Indian divisions are CMM certified to get more project work*"! If the Irish software industry is to compete with those from nations such as India and China radical change is required. The industry itself and indeed those who use software products in their day-to-day business must realise the positive benefits that standardised or structured processes and/ or software quality models can bring not only to the manufacturer of the software but to the user.

From the research conducted within the Irish software community it is evident that a lot of Irish software professionals do not know about process improvement. Management is seemingly ignorant of the benefits that process improvement programs can bring to an organisation. Engineers appear to have a blinkered approach to the process, in that they can only see what is directly in front of them and not the "whole picture".

Companies are focusing on how to fix specific problems "one-at-a –time" including such problems as requirements gathering, issues with estimating projects and poor documentation. Each of these problems can cause serious problems for any organisation if they are not managed correctly. However, standardising the organisation's processes or even following a recognised software process model, can potentially positively impact on each and every one of those problems. It can also bring additional and unforeseen Return On Investment (ROI) benefits to the organisation, as well as demonstrating to potential vendors the maturity and capabilities of the organisation's processes (Goldenson and Gibson, 2003).

If a software quality model is employed, it does not have to be a full implementation of the model. In fact most Small Medium Enterprises (SME's) in Ireland do not have the time, money, or the resources to implement such a model (Richardson, 1999). What has been found within some SME's is that they are successfully *"cherry picking" and tailoring the practices from a variety of software quality models to their own companies existing processes so as to formulate their own "best practices".*

By applying quality models such as the ISO 9000 series of standards or the CMMI it does not necessarily follow that your processes will automatically be improved, nor does it mean that if you apply such models you will gain a considerable return on investment. However it does give organisations a platform upon which to build. Quality models can help focus an organisation towards improving their processes to such a degree that they become standardised, repeatable and maintainable, ultimately leading to profitability. Organisations need more than just a quality model, however. They need to have the right people in place with the right knowledge and experience. They not only need to have the backing of senior management, but they also need senior management to realise the benefits that an improved software process can bring their organisation.

This research is intended to show an alternative to the one-dimensional approach that has apparently been adopted in many Irish software organisations, to date. Some SME's in the Irish software industry cite too little time, money or resources as the prime reason for not examining the potential of a given software quality model while others, simply view such models as *"too much hassle"*. However, there exist those developers who have seen the potential of software quality models, are implementing them and are seeing the benefits, as a consequence. Whether the software quality model chosen is an internationally-recognised model or a tailored, company specific best practices model is not so important. What is important is the desire to improve one's processes on an organisational-wide basis as opposed to a continuous patch-up routine.

Furthermore, this research illustrates that customers generally are not so interested in the quality models in place within the supplier organisations. This is reflected in how often supplier organisations are requested regarding being certified in a particular quality model. Why then should supplier organisations care about such quality models? Suppliers have an obligation to provide quality products. However, they also have an obligation to their owners and shareholders that profits remain high. If suppliers can produce 'good enough' products with no quality model or structured process in place, they will not change their practices unless pressure is exerted upon them. But who is to apply the pressure? Customers do not know enough about quality models to insist on their use. Management will not use them if they do not have to, as they can be considered too expensive. So, how can this situation be changed?

This author feels, that the answer to this question lies in two parts. Firstly, the management in supplier organisations need to be made more aware of quality models and structured processes. They should be made aware not only of the benefits that structured processes can bring, but also of the pitfalls that may be encountered when trying to implement them. Management need to know that quality models can be tailored for use and how to tailor the model or to cherry-pick processes that suit their organisation. Secondly, management should use their structured process or quality models as a marketing tool. Customers need to be educated as to why having structured processes is a good thing for them. If the customer can be shown what benefits models can bring to both they themselves and their supplier, they will carry this knowledge with them to their next purchase.

This could very much be a case of which comes first; i.e. Is it the chicken or the egg? If management are not shown the benefits of quality models, they will not use them, if they can avoid them. If they do not educate their customers about the benefits of quality models or structured processes, customers will not know to ask about them, unless they have had previous experience with processes. So where must the stimulus for change originate from? The author believes that education is the answer.

Members of the Irish software community need to open their eyes to the potential benefits of process improvement programmes. This process must start elsewhere, however. From the research carried out, it was found that only one interviewee in 30 had received no formal third-level education. That leaves 97% of interviewees from varying levels of the management and staff - who have completed some form of third level studies. If 97% of future employees in the Irish software industry could be educated as to the potential benefits of software process improvement initiatives; it would be a good start.

The onus therefore must lie not only with the Irish government who need to continue pursuing a positive economic strategy but also on the third-level institutions that educate our employees. These institutions can affect the future workers in the Irish software industry. If each of these future staff and management members were to be made aware of the potential benefits of software process improvement, they could bring this education with them and positively effect Irish software and non-software organisations alike.

7.4 Advice to Software Firms in Ireland

From the research carried out, it is evident that requirements can cause serious problems for any organisation. Therefore, it would be advisable for organisations, where possible, to involve the customer from a very early stage in the pre-development process. There is a clear need for a well-defined requirements document, but also for customer and senior management sign off on this document. Customers need to be made aware that any change in requirements does not come easy. If possible, changes to requirements should be kept to a minimum, and only allowed in the early stages of the development.

Customers often say when they receive a product "*that's good, but not what I was looking fo*r". Having customers involved from the very start of a project keeps them informed of what is going on, but also gives them a better idea of how it will all turn out. The potential of basic prototyping can be used here and at each development stage. If a customer knows what is going on and can see at each phase how their product is developing, they will be less likely to make major requirements changes as the product develops.

Incorrect estimates were also identified as a serious problem. Developers and (especially) management must retain the knowledge they get from each project and learn as they go on to apply this knowledge to their next endeavour. Problems with estimation can sometimes be traced back to a bad requirements process and poor change management. Companies need to ensure that a proper requirements management process is in place or it will have a negative effect on the estimation process.

Channels of communication between development teams and management must always be open and frequently used. Developers are the ones building the product and are more capable of estimating how long it will take them to do it. However, it is management that set the budget and the timelines. Management need to be aware of potential issues with development as well as taking into account the opinions of their developers when it comes to imposing a deadline.

There is no quick-fix to the issue of documentation use. Some organisations require heavily documented procedures that must be followed. However some other organisations do not need as much documentation, yet may wish to have it. This depends on their management and their employees and how they operate. As with any development project, some individuals need a definite path and structure to follow, while others like a bit of leeway. Documentation can help new people coming in to an organisation, settle in and help them become more productive earlier. At the same time, however, it can hold back other people who just want to get on with the development. However, all employees must know how to use the documentation correctly within any organisation.

7.5 Conclusion

This research was concerned with the discovery of attitudes and experiences of two countries software communities towards the issue of software quality. Research conducted in India appears to show a committed focus on high quality processes. This commitment is not only for the process improvement in itself, but also for marketing and in order to attract continued foreign investment. Research conducted in Ireland suggests a lack of interest in software quality. While some companies have embraced the concepts of software process improvement techniques, others appear either ignorant of its benefits or are simply unwilling to try them out.

In conclusion, the Irish software industry as a whole needs to embrace the concepts of software process improvement and not simply focus on a quick-fix strategy. SPI techniques can help develop quality processes and can be used as a marketing tool to attract and retain customers. More importantly, in a global marketplace where cheap and skilled labour is freely available, quality is becoming a global currency that the Irish software industry can ill-afford to ignore.

BIBLIOGRAPHY

Accenture, (2004). ICT - the Indispensable Sector in the Knowledge Based Economy. Dublin, ICT Ireland.

Allen, G and Skinner, S. (1991) *Handbook for Research Students in the Social Sciences*. London: Falmer Press.

Allgood, B and Rushby, C. (2001). *CMMI: A Comprehensive Overview*. 1st Annual CMMI Tecnhology Conference and User Group. Nov 2001.

Ambler, S. W. (2004). *Tutorial on Aglie Software Development - Are you Agile or Fragile*. EUROSPI 2004, Trondheim, Norway.

Bagchi, S. (1999). "India's Software Industry: the people dimension." IEEE Software Vol. 16(3): 62-65.

Bailey, K. (1994) *Methods of Social Research*. New York: The Free Press.

Bendell, T., (1998). The Quality Gurus: What can they do for your company? London, United Kingdom - Department of Trade and Industry.

Bharati, P. (2005). "India's IT Services Industry: A Comparitive Analysis." IEEE Software Vol. 18(1): 71-75.

Binney, G., (1992). Making Quality Work: Lessons from Europe's Leading Companies. London: Economist Intelligence Unit.

Bollinger, T. B. and C. McGowan (1991). "A Critical Look at Software Capability Evaluations." IEEE 8(2): 25-41.

Buchman, C. D. and L. K. Bramble (1995). "Three-Tiered Software Process Assessment Hierarchy." Software Proccess - Improvement and Practice 1(2).

CAO, (2003). Board of Directors Report 2003. Dublin: Central Applications Office.

Casey, V. B. and I. Richardson (2002). *A Practical Application of the IDEAL Model*. Profes 2002, Rovaniemi, Finland.

Casey, V. B., (2000). The Application of a CMM Based Process Improvement Initiative to a Remotely Located Tool Based Software Application Development Environment. CSIS. Limerick, University of Limerick.

Central_Statistics_Office, (2004). Information Society Statistics - Ireland 2004. Dublin: Government of Ireland 2004: 7.

Clark, B. K., (1997). Effects of Software Process Maturity on Software Development Effort. Faculty of the Graduate School, University of Southern California.

Cohen, L. Manion, L. and Morrisson, K. (2000) *Research Methods in Education*. London: Routledge Falmer.

Crosby, P. (1979). *Quality is Free: The Art of Making Quality Certain*. McGraw-Hill.

Davies, R and Preston, M. (2002) 'An Evaluation of the Impact of Continuing Professional Development on Personal and Professional Lives'. British Journal of In-service Eduction Vol. 28 No.2 pp231-254

Dawood, M. (1994). "It's Time for ISO 9000." Crosstalk: The Journal of Defense Software Engineering (March 1994).

Deming, E. (1986). *Out of the Crisis*. Cambridge, Mass.

DIT, (2005). Annual Report 2004-2005. New Delhi, Indian Department of Information Technology.

EGFSN, (2003). Fourth Report of the Expert Group on Future Skills Needs. Dublin, Forfas - Expert Group on Future Skills Needs.

Enterprise Ireland, (2004). Economic Profile - Ireland. Enterprise Ireland. Dublin, Ireland. Sept04, (2004) 3

Farrell, D., Kaka, N. et al., (2005). Ensuring India's offshoring future. The McKinsey Quarterly, 2005 Special Edition: Fulfilling India's promise.

Farrell, D., T. Khanna, et al., (2004). China and India: The race to growth, The McKinsey Quartely.

Forfas, (2004). Enterprise Strategy Group Report. Dublin: Forfas.

Garvin, D. A. (1984). "What does product quality really mean?" Sloan Management Review 26(1).

Gillies, A. C. (1992). *Software Quality: Theory and Management*. London: Chapman & Hall.

—. (1997). *Software Quality: Theory and Management*. London: International Thomson Computer Press.

Goldenson, D. R. and D. L. Gibson, (2003). Demonstrating the Impact and Benefits of CMMI: An Update and Preliminary Results, Software Engineering Institute.

Graham, R. I. (2002). "ISO 9001:1994 and ISO 9001:2000 compared." IEEE Software Volume 81(Issue 4): 168-169.

Hammersley, M., Gomm, R. and Woods, P. (1994) *Educational research Methods Study Guide*. Milton Keynes: Open University Press.

Heinz, L. (2002). "CMMI Myths and Realities." News @ SEI Interactive 4th Q.

HotOrigin, (2002). Ireland's Software Cluster. Dublin.

Humphrey, W. S. (1988). "Characterising the Software Process: A Maturity Framework." IEEE Software 5(2).

ICT_Ireland, (2005a). ICT sector costs have increased by almost 20% in 2 years. http://www.ictireland.ie/ibec/press/presspublicationsdoclib3.nsf/wvICTNews/BC8ADB4FFD87A57680256FC4003EB612?OpenDocument, ICT Ireland. 2005.

—. (2005b). Key Industry Statistics, ICT Ireland. 2005.

ISA, (2004). Annual Review 2004. Dublin, Irish Software Institute.

Ishikawa, (1985). *What is Total Quality Control? - The Japanese Way*. Prentice Hall

ISO, (1986). ISO 8402:1986

—. (2000). Launching of ISO 9000:2000 series on 15 December. Geneva, International Organization for Standardization.

—. (2002). Joint Auditing Standard for Quality and Environmental Management Systems Now Available, International Organization for Standardization. 2003.

—. (2003b). Selection and Use of the ISO 9000:2000 Family of Standards, International Organization for Standardization.

—. (2003c). ISO's Eight Quality Management Principals. http://www.iso.ch/iso/en/iso9000-14000/iso9000/qmp.html 30/01/2003.

ISO/TC176, (2003b). Frequently Asked Questions, ISO Technical Committee 176. 2003.

Judd, C.M., Smith, E.R., and Kidder, L.H. (1991). *Research Methods in Social Relations*. London: Harcourt Brace Jovanovich College Publishers.

Juran, J. (1979). *Quality Control Handbook.* McGraw-Hill.

—. (1988). *Planning for Quality*. Free Press McMillan.

Kanholm, J. (1999). "A New & Improved ISO 9000." Quality Digest(Oct. 1999).

Keane, B. and I. Richardson, (2004). *Software Quality Models: Decisions by Indian Companies*. European Software Process Improvement (EuroSPI 2004), Trondheim, Norway, Norweigan Technichal University.

King, J. (2002). "How CMM Impacts Quality, Productivity, Rework, and the Bottom Line." Crosstalk: The Journal of Defense Software Engineering(Mar 2002): 9-14.

Kitchenham, B. P., SL (1996). "Software Quality: The Elusive Target." IEEE Software January 1996: 12-21.

Krishnadas, K. C., (2005). India's software exports soar to $12 billion, says Nasscom, EE Times. 2005.

Krueger, R. (1998) 'Analyzing and Reporting Focus Group Results' in The Focus Group Kit. Eds. Morgan, D. and Krueger, R. London: Sage.

Liebesman, S. (2002). *ISO 9000:2000-the challenges and oppertunities for internal auditors*. Annual IEEE Software Conference.

Magnani, G. and I. Garra (1998). *Improvement For The Business*. 4th International Conference on Achieving Quality in Software, Venice.

Marshall, C. and Rossman, G. (1989) *Designing Qualitative Research.* Great Britian: Sage.

McLaughlin, L. (2003). "An Eye on India: Outsourcing Debate Continues." Ieee Software Vol. 20(Iss. 3): 114-117.

McLeod, J. (1999) *Practitioner Research in Counselling.* London: Sage.

Menezes, W. (2002). "To CMMI or Not to CMMI: Issues to Think About." Crosstalk Feb '02.

Moitra, D. (2001). "India's Software Industry." IEEE Software Vol. 18(1): 77-80.

NASA, (2003). Background information on NASA's Quality Management Systems. http://www.hq.nasa.gov/iso/background.doc 30/01/2003.A41

NASSCOM, (2005). Indian Domestic Market: NASSCOM Analysis. New Delhi, National Association of Software and Service Companies.

NCDoT, (2000). Continuous Process Improvement Toolbox, North Carolina Department of Transport (NCDoT)

NSD, (2004). Software Industry Statistics for 1991-2003. http://www.nsd.ie/htm/ssii/stat.htm 15/05/2005. Dublin, Ireland. (2004)

Overby, S., (2004). India Sees IT Wages Rise. CIO Magazine.

Pall, G. A. (1987). *Quality Process Management.* Prentice-Hall.

Parahoo, K., 1997. *Nursing Research: Principles, Process and Issues.* London: MacMillan Press.

Paulk, M. C. (1996). *Effective CMM-Based Process Improvement*. 6th International Conference on Software Quality, Ottawa, Canada.

—. (1997). "Software Process Proverbs." Crosstalk: The Journal of Defense Software Engineering (Jan 1997).

—. (1999). *Analyzing the Conceptual Relationship Between ISO/IEC 15504 (Software Process Assessment) and the Capability Maturity Model for Software*. 1999 International Conference on Software Quality, Cambridge, MA.

Paulk, M. C., B. Curtis, et al. (1993). "Capability Maturity Model, Version 1.1." IEEE Software 10(4): 18-27.

Paulk, M. C., C. V. Weber, et al. (1995a). The capability maturity model: guidelines for improving the software process. Reading, Mass, Addison-Wesley Pub. Co.

Phillips, C. (2005). "Worldwide Tax Overview." Tax Notes International 37(7).

Phillips, M. (2002a). "CMMI Version 1.1: What Has Changed?" Crosstalk: The Journal of Defense Software Engineering (Feb 2002).

—. (2002b). *CMMI V1.1 Tutorial*. European Software Engineering Process Group Conference.

—. (2004). CMMI Combined tutorial. Software Engineering Institute, SEI.

Pitsilis, E. V., J. R. Woetzel, et al., (2004). Checking China's vital signs, McKinsey Quarterly.

Radice, R. A., J. T. Harding, et al. (1985). "A Programming Process Study." IBM Systems Journal 24(2): 297-307.

Reifer, D. J. (2002). "Let the numbers Do the Talking." Crosstalk: The Journal of Defense Software Engineering(Mar 2002): 4-8.

Ribeiro, J., (2005). India's offshore outsourcing revenues grew 34.5 percent, Infoworld. 2005.

Richardson, I. (2001). Software Process Matrix: A Small Company SPI Model. Sofw. Process Improve. Pract. 2001;6: 157-165 (DOI: 10.1002/spip.144)

—. (1999). Improving the Software Process in Small Indigenous Software Development Companies using a model based on Quality Function Deployment. CSIS. Limerick, University of Limerick.

Ryan, Kevin (2005). ISERC special workshop with IPRC. Conrad Hotel, Dublin. 26 August 2005.

Sanders, J. and E. Curran (1994). *Software Quality: A Framework for Success in Software Development and Support*. Reading, Mass., Addison-Wesley Publishing Company.

SEI, (2002a). Overview of the 15504 Collaboration, Software Engineering Institute, Carnegie Mellon.

—. (2002b). Frequently Asked Questions About Sunsetting the SW-CMM, Software Engineering Institute, Carnegie Mellon.

—. (2002c). The SEI Continues Its Commitment to CMMI, Software Engineering Institute, Carnegie Mellon.

SFA, (2005). SFA 11th Annual Employment Survey. Dublin, Small Firms Association.

Sheard, S. A. (1997). "The Frameworks Quagmire, a Brief Look." Crosstalk: The Journal of Defense Software Engineering (Sep 1997).

Shrum, S. (2000). "Choosing a CMMI Model Representation." Crosstalk: The Journal of Defense Software Engineering (Jul 2000).

Silver, B. (1992). "TQM Vs The SEI's Capability Maturity Model." Software Quality World 4(2): 18-26.

Silverman, D. (1995). *Interpreting Qualitative Data: Methods for Analysing Talk, Text and Interaction*. London: Sage Publications

SPICE, (1998a). Software Process Assessment - Part 1: Concepts and introductory guide, ISO/IEC Software Process Assessment.

—. (1998b). Software Process Assessment - Part 2: A model for process management Version 1.00, SPICE.

—. (1998c). Software Process Assessment - Part 7: Guide for use in Process Improvement, SPICE.

Systma, S. and K. Manley, (1999). Quality Tools Cookbook, Ferris State University.

Trauth, E. M., (2000). The Culture of an Information Economy: Influences and Impacts in the Republic of Ireland. Boston, MA.: Kluwer Academic Publishers.

UNCTAD, (2004). World Investment Report - The Shift Towards Services. New York;Geneva, United Nations Conference on Trade and Development.

Webster's. (2003). *Webster's Universal Dictionary and Thesaurus*. New Lanark, Scotland: Geddes & Grosset.

Weinberg, G. M. (1991). *Quality Software Management*. New York: Dorset House Pub.

West, J.E. (2001) Do You Know Your SPC? Quality Digest (July 2001)

Wheeler, D.J. (2000). *Understanding Variation, The Key to Managing Chaos*. Knoxville, Tenn., SPC Press

Wheeler, D.J., T. Pyzdek, et al. (1998). What's in Store for SPC? Quality Digest (Feb. 1998)

Wiegers, K. (1999). "Process Improvement that Works." Software Development(October 1999).

Wilson, N. and McLean, S., (1994) *Questionnaire Design: A Practical Introduction,* Newtown Abbey, Co. Antrim: University of Ulster Press

Zahran, S. (1998). *Software Process Improvement, Practical Guidelines for Business Success*. Addison-Wesley.

APPENDICES

Appendix A – Example of Quality Management Maturity Grid

Measurement Categories	**Stage I: Uncertainty**	**Stage II: Awakening**	**Stage III: Enlightenment**	**Stage IV: Wisdom**	**Stage V: Certainty**
Management understanding and attitude	No comprehension of quality as a management tool. Tend to blame quality department for "quality problems"	Recognising that quality management may be of value but not willing to provide money or time to make it happen.	While going through quality improvement program learn more about quality management; becoming supportive and helpful.	Participating. Understand absolutes of quality management. Recognise their personal role in continuing emphasis.	Consider quality management an essential part of company system.
Quality organisation status	Quality is hidden in manufacturing or engineering departments. Inspection probably not part of organisation. Emphasis on appraisal and sorting.	A stronger quality leader is appointed but main emphasis is still on appraisal and moving the product. Still part of manufacturing or other.	Quality Department reports to top management, all appraisal is incorporated and manager has role in management of company.	Quality manager is an officer of company; effective status reporting and preventative action. Involved with consumer affairs and special assignments.	Quality manager on board of directors. Prevention is main concern. Quality is a thought leader.

Problem handling	Problems are fought as they occur; no resolution; inadequate definition; lots of yelling and accusations	Teams are set up to attack major problems. Long-range solutions are not solicited.	Corrective action communication established. Problems are faced openly and resolved in an orderly way.	Problems are identified early in their development. All functions are open to suggestion and improvement.	Except in the most unusual cases, problems are prevented.
Cost of quality as % of sales	Reported: unknown Actual: 20%	Reported: 3% Actual: 18%	Reported: 8% Actual: 12%	Reported: 6.5% Actual: 8%	Reported: 2.5% Actual: 2.5%
Quality improvement actions	No organised activities. No understanding of such activities.	Trying obvious "motivational" short-range efforts.	Implementation of the 14-step program with thorough understanding and establishment of each step.	Continuing the 14-step program and starting Make Certain	Quality improvement is a normal and continued activity.
Summation of company quality posture	"We don't know why we have problems with quality"	"Is it absolutely necessary to always have problems with quality?"	"Through management commitment and quality improvement we are identifying and resolving our problems"	"Defect prevention is a routine part of our operation"	"We know why we do not have problems with quality"

Appendix B – Capability Maturity Model

Structure of the CMM

Humphrey proposed five maturity levels for the maturity of the software process. A graphical representation of the levels is shown below in figure B.1, which is followed by an explanation of each level.

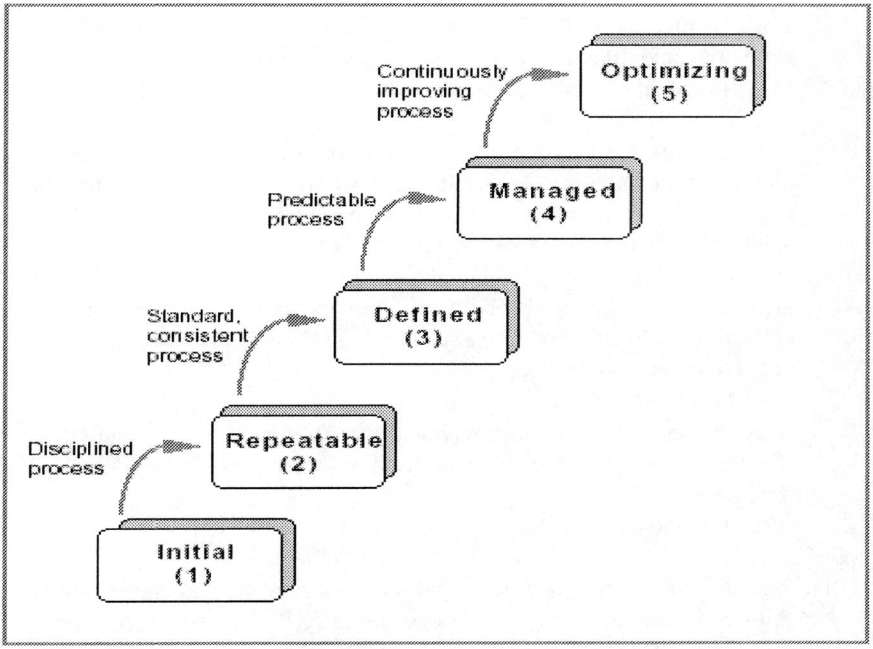

Figure. B.1. The Five Levels of Process Maturity. (Paulk, Curtis et al., 1993)

Organisations must satisfy each criterion of a maturity level before they can be rated as achieving a particular level. The following describes the state of the process at each level.

- *Level 1: Initial* –
  The software process is characterized as ad hoc, and occasionally even chaotic. Few processes are defined, and success depends on individual efforts.
- *Level 2: Repeatable* –

Basic project management processes are established to track cost, schedule, and functionality. The necessary process discipline is in place to repeat earlier successes on projects with similar applications.

- *Level 3: Defined* –

Management and engineering activities are documented, standardized, and integrated into a family of standard software processes for the organization. Projects use a tailored version of the organization's standard software processes for developing and maintaining software.

- *Level 4: Managed* –

Detailed measures of the software process and product quality are collected. Software processes and products are quantitatively understood and controlled.

- *Level 5: Optimising* –

Continuous process improvement is facilitated by quantitative feedback from the process and from piloting innovative ideas and technologies.
(Paulk, 1996)

To be rated at a specific level an organisation has to demonstrate capabilities in a number of key process areas (KPA's) associated with a specific SW-CMM level (Clark, 1997), Defect Prevention is an example of a level 5 KPA, see also Figure B.2. (Richardson, 1999) agrees with this and states that: KPA's identify related activities, that when collectively performed, achieve a set of goals, which enhance process capability.

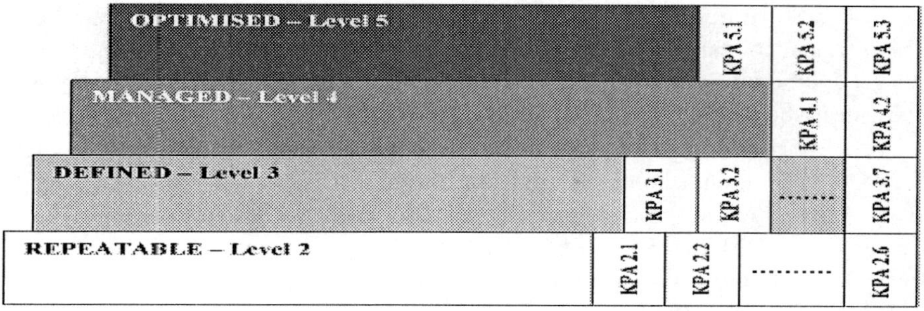

Figure B.2. SW-CMM Maturity Levels and KPA's (Magnani and Garra, 1998)

The key process areas are satisfied by achieving goals, which are described by key practices, sub practices, for examples of the KPA's associated with each level see Figure B.3 (Paulk, 1996). Goals according to Richardson (1999) summarise the practices of each KPA, and are used to assess whether the organisation has in fact successfully implemented the KPA.

Level	Focus	Key Process Areas
5 Optimizing	*Continuous process improvement*	Defect Prevention Technology Change Management Process Change Management
4 Managed	*Product and process quality*	Quantitative Process Management Software Quality Management
3 Defined	*Engineering processes and organizational support*	Organization Process Focus Organization Process Definition Training Program Integrated Software Management Software Product Engineering Intergroup Coordination Peer Reviews
2 Repeatable	*Project management processes*	Requirements Management Software Project Planning Software Project Tracking & Oversight Software Subcontract Management Software Quality Assurance Software Configuration Management
1 Initial	*Competent people and heroics*	

Figure B.3. The Key Process Areas in the SW-CMM (Paulk, 1996)

The Software CMM is referred to as a staged model because it describes organizational capability in terms of maturity levels that represent evolutionary stages of capability" (Paulk, 1999). Paulk goes on to describe a staged model as:

- An organization focused model, since its target is the organization's process capability,
- A descriptive model, because it describes organizations at different levels of achieved capability,

A prescriptive model or normative model, since it prescribes how an organization should improve its process

Advantages of the CMM

The CMM never claimed to be a silver bullet for those organisations seeking to improve their process. It does represent a common sense approach to software development. Using the CMM or indeed any other software quality model will not guarantee success, increased return on investment or reduced defects. However, if used correctly in tandem with other principals including managerial commitment and an educated staff the CMM can help to improve the underlying processes an organisation uses. As it is an internationally recognised standard the use, or rather certification/ maturity rating of an organisation may act as an assurance of sorts for those seeking to do business with a CMM rated organisation. While a particular maturity rating cannot guarantee success it does show a potential client or business partner the ability of an organisation to meet the demands placed on its processes in order to meet an internationally recognised level.

Other, perhaps more concrete advantages have been accredited to the use of the SW-CMM. These advantages include:

- Saved $2 million in first 6 months after reaching CMM ML3 (Sanchez Computer Associates, Inc)
- 15% improvement in internal on-time delivery (Bosch Gasoline Systems)
- Reduction in number and severity of post-release defects (JP Morgan Chase)

Criticisms of the CMM

The staged nature of the CMM is one of its main drawbacks. Even though an organization may have fulfilled each and every KPA from levels 3-5 in the hierarchy, if a single KPA is missing from level 2, then that organization is deemed to be at level 2. Casey (2000) agrees and says that one of the more serious criticisms of the SW-CMM "is the staged nature of the model where achievements at a higher level are ignored if all the other relevant KPA's at lower levels are not addressed.

Another criticism levelled at SW-CMM is that the investment in technology that an organisation makes is very nearly ignored when a company is assessed (Bollinger and McGowan, 1991). Casey (2000) also states that the SW-CMM ignores software product support, an area which Casey goes on to say "is an important element in every software application development cycle, but on the whole remains unaddressed by the SEI. (Silver, 1992) says that the reason that this area is ignored is because the US Department of Defence does not typically include product support.

Paulk cautions against using the CMM for the wrong reasons and states "Standards and models such as the SW-CMM can help organisations improve their software process, but focusing on achieving a maturity level without really improving the underlying process is a danger". He also states that, "Maturity levels should be a measure of improvement not a goal of improvement" (Paulk, 1996). Among other criticism levelled at the towards the CMM were, Initially when the CMM was proposed, there was lots of documentation for assessment followed by some token words about improvement (Richardson, 1999).

Despite the criticisms mentioned above, the SW-CMM can best be summed up by Mark C. Paulk: Paulk (1993) says that the and that "while the CMM is not perfect, it does represent a broad consensus of the software community and is a useful tool for guiding software process improvement efforts (Paulk, Curtis et al., 1993).

Appendix C – Codes from Nvivo

List of codes used in analysis of Irish interviews

- Background
- CMM
- CMMI
- Configuration Management
- Customer_Attitude Customer_
- Complaints Customer_Complaints
- Process Customer_Type
- Design Tools
- Documentation
- Engineers Contribution_Process
- Engineers Contribution_Product
- External Dealings
- GAMP
- Interesting Comment
- Internal Dealings
- ISO 15504 - SPICE
- ISO 9000
- Position
- Process Measurements
- Product Measurements
- Product Quality_BAD
- Product Quality_GOOD
- Product Vs Process Quality
- Quality Definition_Company
- Quality Definition_Personal
- Requirements
- Reviews
- Skills & Resources
- Software Development_General
- Software Development_Problems
- Software Development_Solutions
- Software Process_BAD
- Software Process_GOOD
- Software Quality Definition_Company

- Software Quality Definition_Personal
- Software Quality Models_General
- Software Quality Models_Recommended
- Testing
- Traceability

Appendix D – Concept Note

Concept note - **Customer Driven Process Benchmarking**

The Context

Achieving process excellence in software is the new horizon for the software industry and organizations focus on software process improvements (SPI) and quality models to reach there.

Over the years, multiple models, frameworks, best practices, methodologies, tools and techniques have emerged in the software industry. Today we have a plethora of Quality models (Q models) like CMM, CMMi, ISO 9001, ISO SPICE, SDCE, TickIT, the European Quality Award, Bootstrap, Trillium, ITIL, and the list goes on.

These models address different aspects of the software processes and the organization like development, maintenance, products, security, services, etc. and they all have their specific focus and coverage.

Organizations are faced with a tough challenge on

1. Which Model to adopt
2. How much to adopt (Levels)
3. What should be the timeline

They also need to consider their specific business and organizational needs in evaluating where they stand and what improvement goals should they set.

The intent here is to look at the organization needs in holistic fashion and arrive at the SPI needs in an objective way. In other words, we are looking at an appropriate ***Benchmark*** that organizations can choose before moving forward in their SPI initiative.

Software process Improvement (SPI) and the role of Benchmarking
An increasingly popular way of starting a SPI program is to do a Gap Analysis for determining the current state of the organization's software processes, against a chosen Q Model.

The Trick here is the "what is the correct or appropriate way to benchmark a Q Model before the start of the Gap Analysis"

Why Gap Analysis? And who should do it.

The main reasons to evaluate software processes are:

1. To understand and determine the organization's current software engineering practices
2. To identify strengths, major weaknesses and key areas for software process improvement
3. To facilitate the initiation of process improvement activities
4. To provide a framework for process improvement actions
5. To help obtain commitment, sponsorship and support for action

Not all software units are equally skilled at identifying the causes of their problems or to identify the most rewarding opportunities for improvements. Without a preliminary problem analysis, "solutions" are seldom effective.

What are the different ways of evaluating software processes?

There are two ways in which a software organization can make a preliminary evaluation of its processes and practices:

- Benchmark against other organizations. – To look at the results achieved by some of the best in class companies in the market and the quality models they have adopted. This helps to gain an outside perspective on processes and to borrow ideas and best practices.
- Benchmark against Q models. – This involves evaluating the organizational needs and improvement goals against the tenets and features of existing Q models.

Customer Driven Process Benchmarking Methodology

The objective

To develop a methodology for enabling organizations to make a decision on the most suitable model/models (CMM/CMMi/ISO/ITIL/….) for their software processes.

The Methodology

The methodology will essentially describe, but is not limited to the following:

1. Phases
2. Entry – Tasks – Validation – Exit criteria
3. Work items
4. Work environment aspects – Location, resources, etc
5. People aspects – Roles, Responsibilities, interaction levels, etc

Appendix E – Charter

Charter

What has to be done?

Data Collection - Criteria

Conduct semi-structured interviews to collect data from various organizations regarding factors influencing the selection of a Quality Model.

Factors may include: Budget, Timescale, Contractual Obligations, *Process Properties*, Benchmark against other top companies or simply a desire to improve their overall quality.

The area of Process Properties may be quite large and may have to be investigate in more detail. Which processes were considered? What were the properties of these processes before implementation of the Quality Model? What were the desired levels to be achieved? What levels were actually achieved? Was the implementation considered a Success (rate the success 1-5) What was seen as the reason(s) for Failure/Success?

Once the format of the interview has been decided - it should be piloted/verified within TCS. This will allow for any necessary changes to be made before bringing it to customers. It is then envisaged that we would take this out to customers who have already implemented a quality model and get them to complete it. The more customers we survey means the more accurate any recommendations we make are.

Future work here depends on the completion of the project. After the initial criteria have been selected, they may be continually refined with suggestions from customers or Quality Model experts taken into consideration. Also further surveying of customers where possible to increase accurace and relevance of the information in the database.

Database of criteria

Based on the information collected from the interviews a databse of records must be developed. However further work on this project would include extending it, by including as many projects as possible, thereby refining the tools ability to make accurate decisions. Records/information will be collected via interview/survey this information may be left and analysed as is, or in the future entered into some type of computer database to facilitate ease of record manipulation.

What to we hope to do with the data collected?

Data Analysis

Once the interviews have been conducted and all data gathered, it is hoped that a matrix style framework would be used to analyse the data

This framework, would give the ideal springboard to the development of the decision making tool.

Future Work

Develop the Decision Making Tool

The tool should allow for the entry of criteria and other parameters that will be finalised as research progresses. Based on the information input, the tool should be able to recommend the best or most appropriate Quality Model to implement that will match with Expert opinion.

Timescale

Weeks 1-2: Define what we are to do and how to go about it

Weeks 3-7: Prepare Interview Questions & Data Gathering - conduct interviews with TCS employees and clients/customers

Weeks 8-10: Commence Analysis and development of framework. Identify gaps in data

Weeks 11+: Verify framework with experts in the field

What type of data are we loking to collect? - Interviews

Possible Interview Structure:

TCS is conducting an investigation into the possibility of creating a Customer Driven Decision Making Tool.

The tool's purpose is to aid TCS's customers in the selection of an appropriate Quality Model/Framework to implement. This Interview has been arranged to give us more insight into the process for selecting Quality models.

- Please state the name of your organization
- What type of industry is your organization involved in?
- What is your position in the organization?
- What kind of work do you do?
- What are you currently involved in?
- How long have you worked for the company?
- Have you worked anywhere else?

- What Quality Model was chosen to be implemented?
- If CMM/CMMI, what level was aimed for?
- Were there any Quality Models implemented previous to this one?
- If CMM/CMMI, what level was achieved?
- What were the criteria used to choose this particular Quality Model?
- What reasons had you for choosing these criteria?
- What were the properties of the relevant criteria BEFORE implementation of the model
- Please answer for each criteria?
- What were the DESIRED properties of the relevant criteria BEFORE implementation of the model
- Please answer for each criteria?
- What were the ACHIEVED properties of the relevant criteria AFTER implementation of the model
- Please answer for each criteria?
- What, if any were the reasons for any criteria failing to achieve it's desired level?
- Overall, was the model deemed to have been a success?
- If yes, why was it such a success? If not, why was it not a success?

Appendix F – Methodology Document

Methodology Document

Step 1) Develop Methodology document

Entry Criteria:

Knowledge of what has to be done

Tasks:

Identify scope of project.
Identify steps involved
Estimate Timeframe
Estimate Effort required

Verification:

Present Document to Santosh and Swamy
Refine if necessary until verified

Exit Criteria:

Identified Methodologies, Timeframe and Effort required

Work Products:

Methodology Document Produced

Effort Required by TCS:

Hour long meeting with Santosh, Swamy and myself

Timeframe:

3 Days

Step 2) Develop Data Collection Plan

Entry Criteria:

Received go ahead from Step 1

Tasks:

Determine best way of collecting information
Develop semi-structured interview
Develop Survey questions based on interview
Determine who can be interviewed and (Ideal Minimum 5

Interviews)
Determine who can be surveyed (Ideal Minimum 15-20 Surveys returned)
Determine who the interviewer will be
Determine how to reach the interviewees & those to be surveyed
Secure Services of a Note taker for the interviews (Fluent English/Hindi)

Verification:
Present to Santosh and Swamy
Refine if Necessary until verified

Exit Criteria:
Data Collection Plan Approved
Interviewer, Interviewees and those to be surveyed decided upon

Work Products:
Questions for interview and surveys

Effort Required by TCS:
Hour long meeting with Santosh, Swamy and myself

Timeframe:
1 Week

Step 3) Develop database of Quality Models/Key Process Areas
Entry Criteria:
Received go ahead from Step 1

Tasks:
Identify Quality Models to be included
Identify as many Key Process Areas as possible
Enter information into framework and associate each quality model with relevant KPA's

Verification:
Present to Santosh and Swamy
Refine if necessary until verified

Exit Criteria:

Relevant Quality Models identified
KPA's researched

Work Products:

Framework of Quality Models & KPA's completed

Effort Required by TCS:

Hour long meeting with Santosh, Swamy and myself

Timeframe:

1 Week

Step 4) Pilot Data Collection Plan within TCS

Entry Criteria:

Data Collection Plan developed and approved
Templates include interview and survey questions
Personnel involved identified – interviewer, note taker, interviewees, surveys

Tasks:

Interview & Survey relevant individuals
Enter information into database
Revise questions if necessary

Verification:

All interviews completed
Questions revised if necessary
Present results to Santosh and Swamy

Exit Criteria:

Interviews complete
Information written up on electronic format
Updated questions

Work Products:

Files containing interview information

Effort Required by TCS:

An hour with each individual to be interviewed

An hour and a half of the note takers time per interview
Hour long meeting with Santosh, Swamy and myself

Timeframe:
1 Week

Step 5) Pilot Data Collection Plan within closed group of customers

Entry Criteria:
Data Collection Plan developed, approved & piloted within TCS
Templates include interview and survey questions
Personnel to be interviewed identified
Note taker

Tasks:
Interview & Survey relevant individuals
Enter information into database

Verification:
All interviews completed
Present results to Santosh and Swamy

Exit Criteria:
Interviews complete
Information written up on electronic format

Work Products:
Files containing interview information

Effort Required by TCS/Customer:
An hour with each customer to be interviewed
An hour and a half of the note takers time per interview
Hour long meeting with Santosh, Swamy and myself

Timeframe:
2 Weeks

Step 6) Analyse Pilot Data

Entry Criteria:
Data Collection Plan piloted within TCS

Closed group of customers interviewed
Notes from Interviews with customers and TCS employees written up

Tasks:

Examine collected data for gaps
If gaps determine if those gaps can be filled

Verification:

Present results to Santosh and Swamy

Exit Criteria:

Gaps identified
Measures taken to fill gaps

Work Products:

Complete collection of pilot data from TCS and customer interviews

Effort Required by TCS:

Hour long meeting with Santosh, Swamy and myself
Brief follow up meeting with TCS interviewees may be necessary

Timeframe:

1 Week

Step 7) Refine Methodology

Entry Criteria:

Gaps in data identified
Measures taken to fill gaps

Tasks:

Refine the survey structure to reflect the pilot data analysis

Verification:

Present findings to Santosh and Swamy

Exit Criteria:

Survey refined

Work Products:

Complete survey structure
Updated Quality Model Decision Making Process Document

Effort Required by TCS:

Hour long meeting with Santosh, Swamy and myself

Timeframe:

1 Week

Step 8) Data Collection - Survey to wide group of customers

Entry Criteria:

Data collection plan piloted and refined
Identified those to be surveyed
Identified those to carry out the survey

Tasks:

Carry out surveys with customers
Enter information received in electronic format

Verification:

Files containing the relevant data exist!

Exit Criteria:

A minimum of 20 surveys completed

Work Products:

Files pertaining to each survey stored in electronic format

Effort Required by TCS/customer:

An hour on behalf of customer to fill in survey
Hour and half on behalf of surveyor to complete survey and write up notes
Hour long meeting with Santosh, Swamy and myself ***or*** discussion over phone/email

Timeframe:

3 Weeks

Step 9) Develop framework for information analysis

Entry Criteria:

Some Interviews and Surveys complete, the rest awaiting completion

Tasks:

Develop the framework that will aid in analysis of the information gathered

Verification:

Present to Santosh and Swamy

Exit Criteria:

Framework drawn up

Work Products:

Framework complete with the information gather from interviews and surveys

Effort Required by TCS:

Time to review the framework required of Santosh and Swamy

Timeframe:

2-3 Weeks

Step 10) Analyse information

Entry Criteria:

Framework developed with information gathered from all interviews and surveys

Tasks:

Analyse information

Identify links between criteria selection and successful implementation of Quality Models

Write up report on the information gathered

Write up recommended Methodology document for consultants to use

Verification:

Present work products to Santosh and Swamy

Refine if necessary

Exit Criteria:

Report document finalised
Methodology for consultants finalised

Work Products:

Analysis report

Effort Required by TCS:

Hour long meeting with Santosh, Swamy and myself

Timeframe:

3-4 Weeks

Appendix G – Quality Model Decision Making Process Document

Quality Model Decision Making Process

Table of Contents

I. Overview

The Quality Model Decision Making Process defined in this document is discussed from the Quality Consultant Team perspective. This document focuses on the activities the Quality Consultant Team need to perform using this process.

While this document serves as a navigation tool for the Quality Consultant Team's Quality Model Decision Making Process, it is considered an "evolutionary" document. Continuous enhancement efforts are performed by the Quality Consultant Team to identify lessons learned and incorporate improvements into the process (es).

II. Roles and Responsibilities

The roles and responsibilities defined here are relevant to the Quality Model Decision Making Process.

1. Consultant
    - Gather information on criteria and prioritize them
    - Compare Prioritized Criteria list with list of Ideal Parameters

- Determine best suited Quality Model for implementation
- Determine aspects of other Quality Models that may need to be implemented
- Recommend best suited Quality Model to customer
- Recommend aspects of other Quality Models to customer

2. Customer
   - Select and prioritize criteria for selection
   - Review prioritized criteria list
   - Approve prioritized criteria list
   - Review Quality Model and Aspects recommendation
   - Approve Quality Model and Aspects recommendation

III. Quality Model Decision Making Process

OBJECTIVE:

To support the Quality Consultant Team's efforts to make a customer recommendation as to which Quality Model and which aspects of other Quality Models are best suited to be implemented.

INPUT (S):

- List of questions for customer
- Ideal Parameters for each model
- Criteria Prioritization Report

PROCESS:

Entry Criteria:

- Customer desires TCS to advise on most appropriate Quality Model to implement

Tasks:

- Consultant interviews customer
- Customer specifies relevant criteria and prioritizes them
- Consultant logs prioritized criteria
- Customer reviews and approves/refines log
- Consultant compares prioritized criteria with Ideal Parameters

- Consultant determines best suited Quality Model and other aspects
- Consultant informs customer of recommendation
- Customer reviews/approves recommendation

Validation and Verification:

- Review prioritized criteria log
- Review recommendation

Exit Criteria:

- All criteria specified are covered by recommendation

IV. Output (S)

1. Prioritized criteria log
2. Recommendation

V. Metrics

Metrics to include the following parameters:

- Number of customer criteria versus ideal Quality Model parameters
- Number of aspects of different Quality Models to be implemented

VI. Appendix

Detailed in section II Roles and Responsibilities, the consultant's role refers to

- Gather information on **criteria** and prioritize them
- Compare Prioritized Criteria list with list of **Ideal Parameters**

The "criteria" mentioned above refers to the aspects of the organization and/or organizational processes that are considered by the customer in the selection of the quality Model.

The "Ideal Parameters" mentioned above refers to a template document that is given to the consultant listing the ideal or preferred criteria that each Quality Model values.

The intention here is first the consultant collects the criteria information specified by the customer. Then the consultant will compare the list received from the customer with the template document of quality models and determine from this the most appropriate quality model to be implemented by the customer.

Appendix H – Interview Questions used in India

Data Collection Plan - Interview Questions:

ABC is conducting an investigation into the process for selecting Quality models. This interview has been arranged to give ABC an insight into this process.

Introductory questions:

1. Please state the name of your organization
2. What type of industry is your organization involved in?
3. What is the employee strength of the organization and the geographical distribution?
4. What is the number of IT staff in your organization
5. What is your position in the organization?
6. What kind of work do you do?
7. What are you currently involved in?
8. How long have you worked for the company?
9. Have you worked anywhere else?

Quality Model/Framework Selection Questions:

1. What are/were the primary business concerns that prompted the organization to seek out change in the way that they operated? E.g.: Desire to improve certain processes, Customer Requirement, Contractual obligation, Trade, Desire to increase focus on quality & customer Satisfaction…?
2. What prompted the organization to consider the implementation of a Quality Model/ Framework?
3. What exactly did the organization hope to achieve by implementing such a Quality Model/ Framework?
4. Are there similar effort(s) in other parts of the organization?
5. What knowledge was gained from their experience?
6. What were the top 3 Quality Models/ Frameworks that were considered as possible solutions?
7. Why were these particular models selected for consideration?
8. What other options were considered as potential solutions to the organizations business/ process concerns?
9. What were the criteria used in the selection of the Quality Model(s)/ Framework(s)?
10. Why were these particular criteria chosen?

11. What Quality Model(s)/ Framework(s) were chosen to be implemented? If CMM/CMMI, what level was aimed for?
12. Were any Quality Model(s)/ Framework(s) implemented prior to this one? If CMM/CMMI, what level was achieved?
13. Did the organization choose to implement the chosen model/ framework themselves?
14. Was outside help looked for at any stage?

Quality Model/Framework Implementation Questions:

1. Which 2 or 3 processes was the organization most concerned about prior to implementation?
2. What were the properties of these processes *before* implementation of the model? Please answer for each process?
3. What were the *desired* properties of each process *before* implementation of the model?
4. What were the *achieved* properties of each process *after* implementation of the model?
5. Did each process reach/ surpass its desired level?
6. What, if any were the reasons identified for any process surpassing its desired level?
7. What, if any were the reasons identified for any process failing to achieve its desired level?
8. Overall, was the model/ framework deemed to have been a success? - Why?

Personal Opinion Questions:

1. What do you think makes a process successful?
2. What do you think makes a process less successful?
3. Have you any suggestions on how the *selection* of a Quality Model could be improved?
4. Have you any suggestions on how the *implementation* of a Quality Model could be improved?
5. What difference has the implementation of a Quality Model made on the efficiency of the processes and employees?

Closing Questions:

1. Would you like to ask any questions?

Appendix I – Finalised Questionnaire used in India

Questionnaire to Indian customers

Introductory questions:

1. **What type of industry is your organization involved in? Place an 'X' beside your choice.**

TYPE OF INDUSTRY	'X'
Manufacturing	
Retail	
IT services	
Utilities	
Business Process Outsourcing	
Telecom	
Banking Financial Services	
Others etc	

2. **What is the employee strength of the organization, full time and contractors? Place an 'X' beside your choice.**

FULL TIME EMPLOYEE RANGE	'X'	CONTRACTOR RANGE	'X'
1-50		1-50	
51-100		51-100	
101-500		101-500	
501-1000		501-1000	
Above 1000		Above 1000	

3. What is the approximate number of IT staff in the organization, full time and contractors? Place an 'X' beside your choice.

FULL TIME IT EMPLOYEE RANGE	'X'	CONTRACTOR IT RANGE	'X'
1-50		1-50	
51-100		51-100	
101-500		101-500	
501-1000		501-1000	
Above 1000		Above 1000	

4. What is the geographical distribution of the IT employees?

____

5. What is your role in the organization? Place an 'X' beside your choice.

ROLE	'X'
Chief Executive Officer	
Chief Financial Officer	
Chief Operations Officer	
Chief Information Officer	
Other, Please specify	

6. How long have you worked for the company? Place an 'X' beside your choice.

YEARS EMPLOYED	'X'
0-5	
5-10	
10-15	
Above 15	

7. How long have you been involved in process improvement initiatives? Place an 'X' beside your choice.

YEARS IN PROCESS IMPROVEMENT	'X'
0-5	
5-10	
10-15	
Above 15	

8. Who is responsible for making process improvement decisions within the organization? Place an 'X' beside your choice.

ROLE	'X'
Chief Executive Officer	
Chief Financial Officer	
Chief Operations Officer	
Chief Information Officer	
Quality steering committee	
Other, Please specify	

Quality Model/Framework Selection Questions:

1. **What are/were the primary business concerns that prompted the organization to seek out change? Please rate according to the degree of influence, placing "high", "medium", "moderate" or "low" beside the relevant choices.**

BUSINESS CONCERN	DEGREE OF INFLUENCE
Market need	
Contractual obligation	
Competitive need	
Competitors already implemented it	
Management desire to improve certain processes	
Management desire to increase focus on quality & customer Satisfaction	
Frequent software related problems from production environment	
Trade (Cost effectiveness/ Profitability, Product Quality, Response Time)	
Other, Please specify	

2. **What prompted the organization to consider the implementation of a Quality Model/ Framework? Place an 'X' beside your choice(s).**

WHAT PROMPTED CHANGE	'X'
Internal recommendation	
External recommendation	
Other, please specify	

3. What improvements did the organization hope to achieve by implementing such a Quality Model/ Framework? Please rate according to the most desired improvement, placing "high", "medium", "moderate" or "low" beside the relevant choices.

IMPROVEMENT SOUGHT	DESIRABILITY
Standardization of processes	
Secure customer contract	
Increase customer satisfaction	
Ability to apply for contracts where certain quality model is required	
Improve scheduling	
Improve productivity	
Reduce costs	
Increase product quality	
Improve trace ability	
Improved awareness of quality within the organization	
Other, Please specify	

4. Were any of the options presented below considered as potential solutions to the organizations business/ process concerns? If 'yes', Please specify the options explored.

ALTERNATE SOLUTIONS	'X'
Root cause analysis	
Rational unified process	
Six sigma	
Statistical Process Control	
Other, Please specify	

5. What strategy was implemented when the organization commenced process improvement? Place an 'X' beside your choice(s).

STRATEGIES	'X'
Set of Processes	
All Processes	
Piloting for some Projects and subsequent rollout	
An organization wide improvement approach	
Other, please specify	

6. What Quality Model(s) are currently being implemented in the organization? Place an 'X' beside your choice(s).

MODEL IMPLEMENTED	'X'	LEVEL IF ANY	CERTIFICATION IF ANY
CMM			
CMMI			
ISO 9000:2002			
ISO SPICE			
ITIL			
Trillium			
If other, please specify			

7. Were there any Quality Models implemented previous to this? Place an 'X' beside your choice(s).

MODEL IMPLEMENTED	'X'	LEVEL IF ANY	CERTIFICATION IF ANY
CMM			
CMMI			
ISO 9000:2002			
ISO SPICE			
ITIL			
Trillium			
If other, please specify			

8. In order of importance, what were the influencing factors in the selection of the Quality Model(s)? Please rate according to the most desired improvement, placing "high", "medium", "moderate" or "low" beside the relevant choices. If more than one model was chosen please specify which factor related to which model.

FACTORS	DEGREE OF INFLUENCE	RELATED MODEL
Market entry requirement		
Industry accepted standard/ model		
Cost		
Timeframe		
Organization Size		
Ease of implementation		
Return on Investment		
Technical expertise required		
Internationally recognized standard/ model		
Contractual Obligation		
Process Capability		
If other, please specify		

9. List if any, the specific processes that played a part in the selection of the Quality Model. Please rate according to the most influential, placing "high", "medium", "moderate" or "low" beside the relevant choices.

PROCESSES	DEGREE OF INFLUENCE
Customer supplier process E.g. provide customer service	
Engineering process E.g. develop software requirements	
Support process E.g. perform quality assurance	

Project management process E.g. manage the project	
Organization process E.g. Improve the process	

10. With reference to question 9, what was the improvement noted if any of the chosen processes after implementation of the model?

PROCESSES	IMPROVEMENT NOTED
Customer supplier process	
Engineering process	
Support process	
Project management process	
Organization process	

11. List 3 achievements from the implementation of the model.

ACHIEVEMENTS	'X'
Standardization of processes	
Secure customer contract	
Increase customer satisfaction	
Ability to apply for contracts where certain quality model is required	
Improve scheduling	
Improve productivity	
Improve supplier management	
Reduce costs	
Increase product quality	
Improve trace ability	
Improved awareness of quality within the organization	
Other, Please specify	

12. List 3 difficulties experienced in the implementation of the model.

DIFFICULTIES	'X'
Management commitment	
No clear tangible benefit	
Lack of expertise	
Lack of understanding	
Resistance to change	
Budget overrun	
Timescale overrun	
Unforeseen impact on process	
Others, Please specify	

Additional comments/ information:

Appendix J – Online Questionnaire used in Ireland

Online Questionnaire – Quality Model Adoption Rates in Ireland

This appendix contains complete list of questions from the online questionnaire, used in the Irish research section of this thesis. For the purpose of this thesis, question numbers 2, 3, 7, 10, 11 and 14 were used. These questions are highlighted in **bold** font.

Questionnaire on Quality Model adoption rates amongst the Software Industry in Ireland

1) Please state your name, company and eMail (if you are interested in getting the results)

Name: ____________

Company: ____________

eMail: ____________

2) How many employees are there in your organisation?

- ☐ < 50
- ☐ **50–250**
- ☐ **250-500**
- ☐ **500-1000**
- ☐ **>1000**

3) Are you

- ☐ **an indigenous company?**
- ☐ **a subsidiary of a multinational company?**

4) How many international offices do you currently have?

5)

Are you

- a private company?
- a public company?

6) Which of the following activities is your organisation involved in?

Please rank 1-5 in order of importance (1 = Most Important and 5 = Least)

Product Development

Professional Services

Bespoke Development

Localisation

Hosted Services

7) Is there a dedicated quality manager in your organisation?

- ☐ **Yes**
- ☐ **No**

8) Is process quality and product quality the responsibility of the same person?

- ☐ Yes
- ☐ No
- ☐ Pls expand if No:

9) Which methodologies does your company use to ensure the quality delivery of product and services?

- ☐ We use a formal quality management system
- ☐ We use a formal development methodology
- ☐ We use a formal project management methodology
- ☐ We use a proprietary Project/Development Management methodology

Pls list which methodologies:

10) Which of the following Quality Models have you had experience with:

	No Experience.	Am familiar with concepts.	Have worked with it.	Have evaluated it.	Have implemented it.
ISO 9001:1994	☐	☐	☐	☐	☐
ISO 9001:2000	☐	☐	☐	☐	☐
Malcolm Baldrige National Quality Award (MBNQA)	☐	☐	☐	☐	☐
European Quality Management Award (EQMA)	☐	☐	☐	☐	☐
Deming Application Prize	☐	☐	☐	☐	☐
Capability Maturity Model for Software (SW-CMM)	☐	☐	☐	☐	☐
Capability Maturity Model Integration	☐	☐	☐	☐	☐

(CMMI)					
Spice (ISO15504)	☐	☐	☐	☐	☐
TickIT	☐	☐	☐	☐	☐
Information Technology Information Library (ITIL)	☐	☐	☐	☐	☐
Software Productivity Research (SPR)	☐	☐	☐	☐	☐
Six Sigma	☐	☐	☐	☐	☐
ServQual	☐	☐	☐	☐	☐

11) If you have evaluated any of the models why did you not pursue them?

- ☐ **Not suitable for software development**
- ☐ **Too prescriptive (e.g. detailed, inflexible approach)**
- ☐ **Not prescriptive enough (e.g. too broad, not enough substance)**
- ☐ **Too costly or difficult to implement**

12) Do you have a quality roadmap?

Please Select ▾

13) Are any of the above models on that Roadmap

- ISO 9001:1994
- ISO 9001:2000
- Malcolm Baldrige National Quality Award (MBNQA)
- European Quality Management Award (EQMA)
- Deming Application Prize
- Capability Maturity Model for Software (SW-CMM)
- Capability Maturity Model Integration (CMMI)
- Spice (ISO15504)
- TickIT
- Information Technology Information Library (ITIL)
- Software Productivity Research (SPR)
- Six Sigma
- ServQual

Other (please list):

14) How often are you requested about being certified on a particular quality model during the sales process?

- **0-20%**
- **20%-40%**
- **40%-60%**
- **60%-80%**
- **80%-100%**

15) Have you carried out any of the following activities in the last 2 years in your company?

- ☐ Continuous Improvement Program
- ☐ Quality training to all staff
- ☐ Statistical Process Control
- ☐ Self-Assessment
- ☐ Benchmarking

16) What benefits have the successful implementation of a quality model brought to your organisation

Appendix K – Frequency Tables for Quality Model Experience

Questionnaire – Frequency Tables

Which of the following Quality Models have you had experience with? ISO 9001:1994

		Frequency	Percent	Valid Percent	Cumulative Percent
Valid	No Experience	11	14.3	16.9	16.9
	Familiar With It	13	16.9	20.0	36.9
	Worked With It	16	20.8	24.6	61.5
	Evaluated It	2	2.6	3.1	64.6
	Implemented It	23	29.9	35.4	100.0
	Total	65	84.4	100.0	
Missing	System	12	15.6		
Total		77	100.0		

Appendix L – Publications from this Research

Keane, Brendan and Ita Richardson, Quality: Attitudes and Experience Within the Irish Software Industry, European Software Process Improvement Conference, EuroSPI05, pp 49-58, Budapest, Hungary, 9-11 November, 2005, Lecture Notes in Computer Science, Vol. 3792, 2005, ISBN: 3-540-30286-7.

Keane, Brendan and Ita Richardson "Software Quality Models - Decisions by Indian Companies", EuroSPI 2004 Industrial Proceedings, pp I3-C.15 to I3-C.21, Trondheim, Norway, 9th -11th November 2004.

Appendix L – Publications from this Research

Keane, Brendan and Ita Richardson, Quality: Attitudes and Experience Within the Irish Software Industry, European Software Process Improvement Conference, EuroSPI05, pp 49-58, Budapest, Hungary, 9-11 November, 2005, Lecture Notes in Computer Science, Vol. 3792, 2005, ISBN: 3-540-30286-7.

Keane, Brendan and Ita Richardson "Software Quality Models - Decisions by Indian Companies", EuroSPI 2004 Industrial Proceedings, pp I3-C.15 to I3-C.21, Trondheim, Norway, 9th -11th November 2004.